# An



# THE DIARY OF A YOUNG GIRL

**Eugenie Harris**
Department of English
New York University

This edition published by Barnes & Noble, Inc.,
by arrangement with Macmillan Publishing USA,
a division of Simon & Schuster, Inc.



1998 Barnes & Noble Books



Macmillan Publishing USA
A division of Simon & Schuster, Inc.
1633 Broadway
New York, NY 10019

ISBN 0-7607-1013-9

Text design by Tony Meisel

Printed and bound in the United States of America.

98 99 00 01 02 03 M 9 8 7 6 5 4 3 2 1

RRDC

# CONTENTS

# INTRODUCTION TO ANNE FRANK

## EARLIEST LIFE

Born in Frankfurt am Main, Germany, on June 12, 1929, Annelies Marie Frank was the second daughter of a well-to-do middle-class Jewish family. Her sister, Margot, was three years her senior. Her parents, Otto and Edith came from wealthy families. The Franks lived in Germany, resisting the campaign of the Nazis against the Jews until it was no longer safe to remain there.

## IMMIGRATION TO HOLLAND

When Anne was four, her family moved to Amsterdam, where they lived among the sympathetic Dutch—Christians and Jews alike. Otto Frank prospered as a businessman, and the Franks made many friends—some of whom later risked their lives to protect the family when Germany invaded and occupied Holland.

Anne attended the Montessori School in Amsterdam for six years. Then, in 1940, Jewish children were forced to attend special schools. Anne's transfer to the Jewish Lyceum marks the beginning of a period of increasing difficulty for the Franks and other Jews against whom Hitler's laws were directed. In May of 1940 Germany invaded the Netherlands. The government fled, and in a matter of days all Dutch resistance was crushed except for risky underground activities.

## NAZI OCCUPATION

The discriminatory regulations of National Socialism—Nazism—restricted virtually every privilege of the Jews, from transportation and education to entertainment and commerce. Jews were designated as a separate people by a law requiring them to wear a yellow six-pointed Star of David prominently at all times. The Franks were aware of the temper of the times. Although they continued for two more years to live what was on the surface a normal life, Otto Frank and a group of friends were making plans for their survival. Each day strands of an invisible web being woven about the group in preparation for their eventual "disappearance." The choice would soon have to be made—whether to risk arrest and removal to concentration camps, or to take matters into their own hands and hide, as flight from Nazi-infested Europe was no longer possible. With the Gestapo (Hitler's police force) stalking the streets of Amsterdam in search of Jews whom they "summoned" on the flimsiest pretext, July 1942 brought fulfillment to the Franks' plans.

## IN HIDING

On July 9 the family embarked on their last free walk along the streets of Amsterdam. In an ordinary manner, so as not to arouse suspicion, they greeted people they knew. Wearing layer upon layer of clothes, and carrying satchels filled with belongings, they journeyed in a pouring summer rain the short distance to their hiding place, an office building. At the rear of the third and fourth floors was a hidden apartment in which the Franks, another family named van Daan, and Alfred Dussel remained in exile for the next two years. It is during this period that Anne wrote her diary, which reveals an extraordinary literary talent for one so young and provided the world with a valuable document of World War II.

## DISCOVERED

On August 4, 1944, the Gestapo raided the apartment hideout. They searched the quarters, confiscating anything they considered of value. The diary was spilled out of Otto Frank's briefcase along with other papers the Gestapo considered unimportant. It lay on the floor among a pile of books and papers until found later by friends who preserved it. All of the occupants of the apartment were arrested and sent to German concentration camps. Of these eight people, only Otto Frank survived. Two of the friends who had served as links to the outside were also arrested and sent to a Dutch concentration camp. Enduring their imprisonment, they were able to return to their families. Anne herself died at Bergen-Belsen, a German concentration camp, in February or March, 1945, just two months before both her sixteenth birthday and the Allied liberation.

## HOW AND WHY IT HAPPENED

If there is any explanation for the atrocities committed during World War II by the Hitler regime (the Third Reich), it lies in historical facts that combined freakishly to produce such acts on the parts of many people. An understanding is required of social and economic conditions that constitute the underlying causes of war before the immediate causes can begin to be understood. Once war has begun, the actions of all people involved often lie beyond moral or rational considerations. There is no suitable answer to "why" in cases like that of Anne Frank and her family. Nevertheless, a brief look at the conditions that gave rise to the fanatical Adolf Hitler will help.

# HISTORICAL BACKGROUND

## ECONOMICS

Although all European countries were hard hit after 1929 by a general economic depression, the plight of Germany was the worst. The Versailles Treaty of 1919, which ended World War I, had left Germany economically crippled as punishment for being guilty of the war according to the victor nations. Stripped of her colonial possessions and humiliated, she was saddled with enormous reparations payments to the Allies. While England and the United States sought a compromise in the making of payments so that Germany could restore a degree of economic health, France and Belgium punished their neighbor for defaulting by occupying the industrial section of Germany known as the Ruhr. World economic conditions were such that strikes occurred among workers of all nations. When German workers acted similarly and production of goods ceased, Germany declared bankruptcy. An international committee was set up to consider the problem. The result was the adoption of the Dawes Plan, which enabled Germany to borrow money from other countries and stabilize finances. When she did again begin to make reparation payments, France and Belgium withdrew their troops from the Ruhr. There was still considerable pressure on Germany to keep up her payments to the other Allies, who owed money to the United States for loans made to finance World War I. Germany was in a serious economic bind.

## POLITICS

The trend in Europe after World War I was one of liberalism and democratic government. In 1918 the empire ended in Germany when local princes abdicated. In 1919 the formation of the Weimar Republic was accomplished by the ratification of a democratic constitution. This did not guarantee peace from within, as factions on the left and right still struggled for power. There was dissatisfaction over the humiliations suffered by Germany under the Treaty of Versailles. Revolts were common. By 1928 much of this inner turmoil had been settled, and Germany was beginning to see daylight with Paul von Hindenburg, initially a capable man, as president. After the onset of the 1929 depression, extremist groups once again rattled the political stability of the republic.

## HITLER'S RISE

Economic threats caused panic among splintering groups of German citizens, whose only common goal was security and stability. Such social and economic instability brought about a loss of faith in the Weimar Republic and in the capability of its aging president, Hindenburg. Renewed bitterness against the Versailles Treaty, which he continued to support, paved the way for the spread of a fanatical nationalism. Embodying this spirit was Adolf Hitler, a maladjusted World War I veteran who harbored a maniacal hatred for democracy, trade unions, Jews, and Communists. His National Social German Workers' (Nazi) Party had attempted in 1923 to seize power from the shaky young Weimar Republic, but the plot had failed and he had been imprisoned. In 1929, however, conditions were ripe for Hitler, whose hypnotic powers of persuasion could sway a frightened and disillusioned people. The Nazi party's growth was spectacular, and by 1933 Hitler had gained enough popular support for a reluctant Hindenburg to entrust him with the post of chancellor. From this point on, the usurpation of control was easy, and Hitler lost no time in establishing his dictatorship.

## HITLER'S PROGRAM

Hitler's avowed purpose was to reestablish Germany's power and prestige and restore economic stability by reviving industry and agriculture. His terms for achieving this were based on three main objectives: (1) the negation of the Versailles Treaty; (2) the creation of a strong economic and military Germany; and (3) the elimination of Communist, Jewish, and all other "non-German" interests. This program appealed widely to a proud people brought to its knees by international degradation and economic chaos. German youth were especially receptive to Hitler's plans, for they had known little if anything of German glory in their lifetimes. If some members of the older generation were reluctant to embrace the fanatical surge of this new nationalism, they maintained an attitude of indifference or passive acceptance for a while, feeling that social and economic conditions warranted improvement by almost any workable means. But soon it became apparent that the only attitude possible under the Hitler regime was acceptance and willing participation whether out of enthusiasm or fear. For in June 1934, the people were taught an object lesson in the execution of some few hundred suspected by Hitler of opposition to his program.

## HITLER'S INFORMATION SERVICE

Hitler's public relations policy seemed to be everywhere at once. Enlarged photographs of the führer were inescapable, as were swastikas (the Nazi emblem). Having seized control of mass communications early in his dictatorship, Hitler was able to suppress any information that might threaten the Reich's policies and to spread those ideas which would benefit them. In these ways he forced adherence to his program by controlling the thinking of an entire nation. As time went on, the methods and activities of the Nazis developed inhuman aspects. Nevertheless, such distorted information was disseminated concerning these horrors that many Germans were only vaguely aware of what was actually happening. The outside world also knew little. Except for rumors, only Hitler and his closest henchmen—who were sworn to secrecy—knew what was in store for those out of favor with the Reich.

## PREJUDICE AND PERSECUTION

Hitler was a powerful orator with an ability to rouse people to frenzied action. He shrewdly exploited nationalistic sentiment by making his own distorted desires appear to be the goals of Germany. His ability to twist historical facts enabled him to convince the masses that Jews, Communists, Socialists, and Catholics were responsible for Germany's misfortunes. Jews, he maintained, had encouraged acceptance of the Versailles Treaty in order to protect their economic interests abroad and to wring profit from the war debt. He emphasized that Jews were not truly of German blood and could never be considered loyal Germans. The Communists were Hitler's political opponents, and he stressed their affiliations with the Soviets, thus making them into agents of foreign interests. Socialists, too, were discredited and vilified as part of an international movement. The Catholics' religious loyalty to Rome was the issue he exploited where that group was concerned. Hitler's aim was to "purify" the German population of these and all so-called non-Aryan elements. By attributing the ills of the nation to them he efficiently made these groups the national scapegoat. With the temper of the people inflamed, he could do whatever he wanted and count on support.

## FOREIGN POLICY AND WAR

Information leaked out of Germany concerning internal affairs horrified the world, but no one was brave enough to antagonize this powerful dictator so long as he kept his activities confined within his own country. Appalled by bits and pieces of news about the fate of a few unfortunate individuals, the Allies were more concerned with the disturbing advent of totalitarian governments in Italy, Russia, and Japan. These dictatorships, along with Germany, threatened to upset the status quo. It was hoped that the League of Nations could preserve the peace in Europe. The Geneva Disarmament Conference of 1932–1934 was intended to correct the failure to disarm those nations that had promised to disarm in the Versailles Treaty. Alarmed at the menace presented by the potential military strength of the Third Reich, these nations could not come to any terms of agreement on arms reduction at the sacrifice of their safety. In 1933 Hitler blasted all hopes for an easing of European tensions by withdrawing from both the Geneva Conference and the League of Nations. In 1935 he announced Germany's intention to rearm. Still nervous about the Reich's lack of a strong European ally, he held his aggressive aspirations in check until an agreement known as the Axis was established with Italy in 1936.

Nazi infiltration into countries where German minorities existed had been in progress since 1933. Hitler's aim was to unite all German peoples into a "Greater Germany," comprised of the German-populated areas of other European countries, and ultimately to wield total authority from Berlin. In March 1938 Austria became a German province. In September of that year he annexed the Sudetenland portion of Czechoslovakia, and in April 1939 proclaimed another portion of that country a German protectorate. Having agreed to divide Poland with Russia, in September 1939 Germany invaded Poland. The result of the invasion was the declaration of war on Germany by the French and British. In April 1940 Hitler's troops accomplished the occupation of Denmark and Norway in a single day. In May the Germans invaded Belgium and the Netherlands. The Dutch resistance lasted four days, whereupon Queen Wilhelmina and the government fled to England. The Belgians held out for eighteen days under King Leopold. By June, Hitler had subdued France and established the Occupational (Vichy) government of Pétain. These battles constituted the early stages of World War II.

## PINPOINTING THE JEWS

As early as 1933, the Jews in Germany were victimized by discriminatory legislation. Their position was reduced over the next six years from secondary citizenship to noncitizenship, and finally to virtual nonexistence. The "Jewish Question" was an issue carried over from the early days of the Nazi party's program of 1920. More than simply an aspect of early Nazism, to Hitler a solution to the Jewish Question was a goal of paramount importance. As anti-Jewish legislation became an increasing reality in Germany, many Jews left the country. More Jews, however, remained, thinking that the current lenient emigration policy would continue. On the basis of family ties, wealth, possessions, and careers, there was less of a desire to emigrate than to endure current discrimination. Many Jews even looked on Germany as their homeland and felt, as "true" Germans, that the measures of the Nazis were temporary.

## THE FIRST SOLUTION

In 1938 the "First Solution" to the Jewish Question was enacted with startling swiftness. In a word, it was expulsion. The wealthier Jews had little difficulty in leaving; the poorer ones could not so easily afford the costs of proper documents or transportation. With only two weeks allotted them to emigrate, less affluent people looked for guidance to Jewish functionaries working with the Nazis on relocation. The black marketing of passports was on the rise, as were bribery, forgery, theft, and other measures necessarily taken by those with a price on their heads. Some Jews attempted to renounce their religion, either by conversion or by falsified birth certificates. Others were willing to remain in Germany whatever the penalty if just one family member's salvation could be assured. Escape by underground methods became frequent.

In the early days of emigration, Jews had found it relatively easy to relocate to neighboring nations such as Holland, Belgium, France, and England. Some scattered to Scandinavia or British-held Palestine, and even to Canada, South America, and the United States. Some difficulties were connected with the immigration laws of their adopted countries, but for the most part, the early émigrés were rather easily resettled. After the 1938 decree, the wealthier Jews found relocation more difficult, and the poorer Jews found it virtually impossible. The officials of the Jewish communities, Jews themselves, arbitrarily selected destinations that, as often as not, were considered worse than remaining in Germany. Torn between the alternatives offered by their own leaders and the Nazis, these individuals were helpless and stranded.

## THE SECOND SOLUTION

With too many Jews remaining in Germany to suit him, Hitler enacted what he termed the "Second Solution." Between 1938 and 1939, those who could procure no papers or find no place of relocation or were still in Germany for some other reason were sent to concentration camps until their fate could be decided. Many Jews hid, aided by sympathetic friends and neighbors. The Jewish functionaries who felt exempt from danger by virtue of their work for the Reich, and who for a while longer believed that they were helping their people to avoid committing crimes against the administration, sought out fellow Jews in hiding and rounded them up for the concentration camps. Sympathizers, when discovered, were punished as political criminals and likewise deported to the camps.

## THE CAMPS

Little was known about the concentration camps at first, except that for Jews remaining in Germany they were temporary locations. It was thought that perhaps German penal colonies in remote regions of the globe would be established as a possible answer to the problem of relocation. Meanwhile, those in the camps were forced to work if they were strong and healthy, or subjected to brutality and perversion if they were not. Prisoners of all ages were herded across Europe to the camps in cattle cars. Upon arrival they were segregated according to the function in which they could best serve the Reich. Family ties and other human considerations meant nothing. The weakest died first. Conditions for survival were at a minimum. Germany could not afford to "waste" food, clothing, and medicine on Jews. Prisoners suffering from malnutrition or disease were the victims of "mercy killings."

## THE FINAL SOLUTION

By 1939 Hitler's aggressive tactics in international affairs had plunged Germany into the initial phases of World War II. Wartime economy as well as war psychology demanded a "Final Solution" to the "Jewish Question." This meant extermination. All Jews in Germany and German-occupied countries were to be killed. "Experts" on the Jewish Question such as Adolf Eichmann were consulted. Removal of the Jews to remote places was now a discarded plan because of the impossibilities of wartime transportation. Under Hitler's orders all Jews were to be rounded up and sent to certain camps where special equipment was being built for their extermination. The "Final Solution" went into effect in 1941.

Enormous gas chambers were constructed to resemble ordinary buildings large enough to contain hundreds, and in some cases thousands, of people. These buildings contained outlets for the poison gas that would be piped in and controlled from the outside by valves. In a few hours, when asphyxiation was complete, the corpses were removed and a new batch of prisoners who had been promised "showers" before relocating were locked in for the next gassing. The disposal of the corpses presented another problem, as burying thousands of bodies was impractical. So cremating the remains was decided on. Huge crematoriums were erected near the gas chambers.

## OCCUPIED HOLLAND AND THE JEWS

The Jewish population of the Netherlands in 1942 was approximately one hundred and forty thousand. Of these, some thirty-five thousand were "stateless" Jews, which meant that they were refugees, mostly from Germany. The

Dutch had been openly hostile to the anti-Jewish measures taken by the Nazis since the occupation of Holland in 1940. When, in 1942, the programming of the "Final Solution" went into effect in the Netherlands, it meant the initial deportation of twenty thousand Jews to concentration camps. This enactment resulted in violent opposition among the Dutch in the form of a wave of strikes.

The Dutch sympathy for the Jews was threatened in two ways. First, that segment of the population involved in the Nazi movement formed a very powerful machine. The Dutch Nazis could be counted on to unearth Jews from their hiding places, after which seizure and deportation were carried out. Second, among the Jews themselves, there existed a split between the native-born and the refugees. The native Jews were led to believe that it was only the foreigners who were to be the victims of Hitler's plans. To save themselves, many Dutch-born Jews were enlisted by the Nazis into a Jewish police force. This pitting of Jew against Jew resulted in the deportation by July 1944 of one hundred and thirteen thousand Jews. This figure included a large percentage of native Dutch Jews whose collaboration with the Nazis proved a catastrophe out of proportion to anything these duped people could possibly have imagined. For even among the twenty thousand Jews who survived in hiding, only five thousand were Dutch born.

# INTRODUCTION TO
# *THE DIARY OF A YOUNG GIRL*

William Wordsworth wrote in his "Intimations of Immortality" of the unusual perception of children: "Mighty Prophet! Seer blest!/ On whom those truths do rest/ which we are toiling all our lives to find." These lines pertain well to Anne Frank, an average teenager confiding her most private thoughts to her diary, a make-believe friend she had named Kitty. Groping her way through the confused years of early adolescence, Anne was not only brave enough to ask why regarding the ways of human nature but also perceptive enough to begin ferreting out some of the most important answers to questions all people ask themselves about their fellow creatures.

Ironically aided by the conditions of war, Anne observed humankind's rawest acts. She was able to formulate conclusions regarding the nature of people generally as well as under duress. What was remarkable was her ability to handle some of the most complicated answers to life's questions—questions that even many adults do not wish to consider. She also possessed heroic strength in being able both to find and accept the truth. For despite the tendency of the young to keep the self exclusively in focus, Anne's vision was broad enough to include a field of relationships, broadening from those of immediate family and companions to humanity as a whole. Aside from an uncommon awareness, she had an exceptional ability to judge herself and others with an untutored wisdom.

What evolves from the pages of Anne's diary is a philosophy of life rare not only for such a young person but for any individual subjected to the ugliness of war. Threats to existence and the human spirit do not ordinarily produce the positive attitude with which Anne faced her circumstances.

It was the will not only to go on in a semiexistence diseased by fear, but to go on making every moment count, and above all, to survive beyond the moment. Despite the horrors and humiliations of each day, the constantly alternating factors of salvation and disaster, and the unbalanced elements of good and evil, Anne's was a spiritual force of unusual drive and direction. Such spiritual strength occurs only in individuals of rich inner resources.

Because Anne's work is a diary, we might best call it a self-portrait, which must include a self-interpretation. Because she is young, she is apt to see herself both factually and fancifully. All the elements of her life become incorporated into the portrait: her family, her immediate associates, the war, the temper of the times. We sympathize with her problems of growing up. We understand that because of her age there are occasional distortions in her perspective. Her discoveries about life may be things we already know. Where she is naive, we may chuckle. Where she becomes profound in her observations of humanity, we may be astonished at her wisdom. In her analysis of herself and others, she may be harsh at times and awkward at others. Because this work is a diary, it concentrates on the little details of daily life, and in Anne's case, it is an unusually limited routine because of the confinements of the Franks' hiding place. But because Anne is an imaginative young person, she is able to delve deeply into a small environment and broaden its confines with a richness of detail beyond the scope of the ordinary observer. These are the elements that combine to produce a portrait of great depth and dimension.

## A NOTE ON STYLE

Anne Frank was thirteen when she made the first entry in her diary and fifteen when she wrote the last. An unpracticed writer, save for training in composition at school, she saw the diary as a means of unburdening her innermost thoughts to an imaginary friend named Kitty. Of course, Kitty was the sort of friend who would have the most sympathetic response to Anne—an ideal confidante whose patience and understanding were guaranteed. Because there could be no opposition from Kitty to Anne's thoughts, the young writer could safely and privately give voice to her most honest self. Therefore, Anne could also experiment with her writing. The first entries are formally composed and somewhat self-conscious in their labored correctness. As the diary progresses, Anne seems to fall into an easier, more conversational style, identifiable by better-turned but less rigidly constructed sentences. There is also a frequent easing into casual language. Besides style, the content develops throughout the pages. The author loses her inhibitions, unmasking more and more facets of her personality. The process is clearly one of self-discovery developing through the honest expression of her thoughts. The range is what might be expected from a girl of Anne's age—doubt, introspection, criticism, analysis, observation—all directed toward the goal of getting to know herself.

Despite the fact that both the style and content show Anne's increasing maturity throughout the diary, there is a general lack of the artificial touches used by older authors to screen their true characters from the reading public. Anne's straightforward expression is in evidence continually as she writes of matters both within herself and without. Sensitive to all things, she endows each entry with intensely personal and human expression, that manner of writing so like the self's own voice that many professional writers often fail to achieve. What also bears consideration is the great potential Anne's work reveals. For, had she lived to continue with her writing, as she expected, she planned to be a professional writer. Such characteristics as her ability to detach herself as an observer, her skill in recording both the scenes of her external life and the complexities within herself, indicate the presence of remarkable talent. Her philosophical comments and injections of humor contribute to the high appraisal placed on her work.

## ANNE FRANK AND HISTORY

"I believe in the good of man," wrote a young girl in her diary, a girl experiencing the dehumanizing effects of a man whose slogan was "My mission is to destroy and exterminate." The girl was a young Jew named Anne Frank; the man tormenting her and her people was a dictator named Adolf Hitler. He succeeded in his mission to a great extent but lost his cause in its entirety. His failure is the recorded history of World War II, and one document in its myriad testimony is *The Diary of a Young Girl.*

As a document of World War II, Anne's diary has helped bring judgment against the Nazi persecutors of Hitler's machine. As a work of literature, it has brought renewed inspiration to those who survived the Third Reich's atrocities. Moreover, the little journal has kept alive the spirit of an exceptional young person whose thoughts have broadened the perspective of millions of readers of all ages. Transcending nationality, race, and religion, *The Diary of a Young Girl* has been published throughout the world, including Germany. From its humble origins, it has become a monument to the human spirit, a continuing affirmation of humankind's destiny to survive, and the triumph of good over evil.

# DETAILED ANALYSIS

## JUNE 12, 1942–JULY 8, 1942: LIFE ON THE OUTSIDE

Of the many gifts Anne Frank receives for her thirteenth birthday, the one she values most is a diary. Longing for the sort of friend with whom she can share everything, Anne names the diary Kitty, declaring that the entries will be in the form of letters to her newly created confidante. Anne's purpose in writing these letters is more than just to report day-to-day occurrences. Her intention is to reveal herself totally, unburdening all her thoughts and discussing her experiences at length.

Having stated her purpose in keeping the diary, Anne sketches briefly her autobiography. She tells Kitty how her family—father, mother, and older sister Margot—came to Holland in 1933 from Germany to escape the early persecution of the Jews by Hitler. All went well until 1940, when the Nazis conquered the Netherlands. Under Nazi occupation, the situation of the Jews even in Holland has grown increasingly unpleasant because of the anti-Jewish laws imposed by Hitler. Jews are banned from most modes of public and private transportation, forbidden to attend all places of public entertainment, and prohibited from participation in all public sports. Jews are permitted to shop only in specially designated stores and only at prescribed hours. Jews must attend special schools, be inside their homes by 8:00 P.M., and wear the mark of their religion—a yellow six-pointed Star of David—prominently on their persons at all times.

In spite of these restrictions, Anne finds pleasure in life through school, relationships with her friends, reading, playing Ping-Pong, and her family. At the Jewish Lyceum that Anne and Margot have attended since being required to withdraw from the Montessori School, there is great excitement over who will move up to the next form after the examinations. Anne comments to Kitty on the eccentricities of teachers and the intelligence or lack of it among her schoolmates. She describes her own bad habit of being a chatterbox, for which she has been reprimanded at school. Anne also discusses her boyfriends and her flirtatious nature, describing with pleasure the ups and downs of popularity with the opposite sex. She secretly favors Peter Schiff but receives more attention from others, notably a boy of sixteen named Helmuth (Hello) Silberberg. Hello is an immigrant from Belgium and lives with his grandparents, who object to his seeing so much of a girl Anne's age. Nevertheless, Hello is well received at the Franks' home, and despite his youthful seriousness, Anne admits that while she enjoys his attentions and his company, she is not in love with him. Anne also writes with nostalgia of Grandma, Mrs. Frank's mother, who came to live with the family in 1938 and died in 1942.

Anne learns from her father that there are plans afoot for the family to go into hiding. For over a year the Franks have been distributing their possessions among Christian friends to avoid having them seized by the Germans. Recently Mr. Frank has withdrawn from active participation in his business, leaving in charge two trusted associates, Mr. Kleiman and Mr. Kugler. In recent weeks the SS (Secret Police) has been issuing more frequent call-ups for many Jews, which result in arrest and deportation. Because it is no longer possible either to leave Holland or to remain safely in their present mode of life, the only alternative for the Franks is to go into hiding. Plans and preparations have been made for this eventuality by the Franks and another family, the van Daans. Aided by close friends who are also business associates, a "disappearance" has been arranged and a hiding place prepared. Aside from Kleiman and Kugler, the collaborators in the plan are Miep and Jan Gies and Bep Voskuijl, a secretary. A call-up for Margot triggers the disappearance of the Franks a week ahead of schedule. The family is evacuated from their home in a matter of hours.

Once things have calmed down enough to permit Anne to write in her diary, she describes the evacuation procedures to Kitty. From the moment of the call-up for Margot, the Frank household began proceeding with emergency measures. Throughout the day and much of the night Miep and Jan made several trips from the Franks' house to the hiding place. On each trip their pockets and satchels were crammed full of the Franks' possessions—such small articles of personal effects, food, and clothing as could be transported without arousing curiosity. The Franks themselves had hardly any sleep, arising at 5:30 A.M. and leaving things in disarray two hours later.

## JULY 9, 1942–JUNE 15, 1943: THE FIRST YEAR

For Anne, the beginning of their new life seems like a vacation at a strange inn where the guests live in a nervous atmosphere of odd silence and necessary but peculiar rules. During the day all must be quiet so that no one employed downstairs or in the neighboring buildings will suspect their presence. Curtains, crudely made by Anne and her father, now cover the windows and will never be taken down until the period of hiding is over. Minor decorations adorn the walls in an attempt to make the place seem more cheerful. Nevertheless, Anne finds the silence very frightening, and even more oppressive is the notion that she can never go outdoors. The fear of discovery underlies every action and is a constant source of tension.

Within three days the van Daan family arrives—husband, wife, and sixteen-year-old son Peter. The Franks are relieved to learn that everyone on the outside has a different theory regarding their disappearance. Even Mr. Goldschmidt, a lodger in the Franks' former home, has been tricked into thinking that they have escaped to Switzerland. It does not take long, however, for the seven inhabitants to develop little tensions, first within their own families and then between members of the other group. Mrs. Frank and Mrs. van Daan develop a petty rivalry over utensils and other communal household supplies. Anne finds herself easily upset by her own mother and the van Daans, except for Peter who manages to stay out of everyone's way. Mr. and Mrs. van Daan quarrel in a way that the Franks find both appalling and amusing. Anne begins to recognize the difference in the standards and values of the two families and the difficulties of adjustment. As the realities of the confinement become more apparent through the limited routine of daily life, so do each person's selfish tendencies. Bickering and tears are not uncommon.

Although Anne has taken a holiday from studies until September, she and the others read a great deal to occupy their time. Mr. Kleiman brings new books each Saturday. Some are considered too adult for Anne and Peter at this time, and incidents regarding forbidden reading matter occur as a result. Aside from household duties, an activity shared by all is listening to the radio downstairs in the private office in the evening when no one is about. Although it is illegal to have the dial turned to any station other than a German one, the group listens only to broadcasts of music on that station, for other Nazi programs are too hateful and depressing. They prefer the newscasts and other programs of the BBC (English), which are more encouraging. Queen Wilhelmina of the Netherlands often sends messages to her subjects over the airwaves from England, where she and her family are in exile. The occupants also take heart from Winston Churchill's speeches.

The families receive their food and other supplies from their protectors, Miep, Jan, Bep, Mr. Kleiman, and Mr. Kugler. They have been able to purchase extra ration books on the black market, and their food supply is adequate. An added security measure is the building of a sliding cupboard in front of the doorway leading to the hidden apartment. Through this disguised doorway come their allies on visits, bringing supplies as well as news and encouragement. Except for the footsteps of these trusted friends, other noises in the building at the wrong hours bring terror to the hearts of all. One such incident occurs when Kleiman's rapping on the door is thought to be that of a workman who has come to fix the fire extinguishers. The three days during which a plumber is making repairs are also anxious ones, as no water facilities may be used nor may there be any activity at all during his working hours downstairs. One particularly tense moment comes with the inspection of the building by a new owner. Kleiman is obliged to show him the premises. He pretends to have forgotten the key to the doorway leading to the secret portion in back of the private office. Fortunately, he is not questioned by the new owner.

An eighth person is added to the group, Alfred Dussel, a Jewish dentist. Anne has her reservations about sharing a room with him, but such arrangements are not ones of choice. Dussel is amazed at the elaborate system of living accommodations in the hiding place. Although their protectors have held back many of the ugly details of life on the outside, the group's curiosity is so persistent that Dussel reveals many of the Nazi activities that have taken place since the group has been in hiding. Particularly terrifying are the reports of Jews being deported and sent to their deaths, many of whom were friends and acquaintances of the occupants. Mr. Dussel, in turn, is rather stunned by the quarrels that seem never to cease among those in the hideout. He attempts to ignore the tension by pursuing his own interests.

Anne writes extensively about the personality conflicts, many of which involve her in one way or another. The van Daans and Dussel think she is spoiled by her parents. She and her mother are constantly on bad terms. Margot and

Anne also have their differences. The result is that Anne usually seeks justification from her father, whose method of arbitration is one of judicious sympathy for Anne coupled with a gentle elucidation of her faults. Mr. Frank will not become too strong an ally of anyone in these battles. Mrs. van Daan and Mrs. Frank have growing tensions, not only from conflicts over communal supplies and differing values but also because Mrs. van Daan attempts to flirt with both Mr. Frank and Mr. Dussel. Anne and Mrs. van Daan do not always get on well, for the older woman's disapproval of the girl's upbringing is one of her favorite topics. This often brings the van Daans and the Franks into larger disagreements. Mr. and Mrs. van Daan quarrel regularly in unpleasant terms and tones of voice. Mr. Dussel has his irritating little ways, one of which is siding with Anne's critics. Arbitration in most of these matters comes from Mr. Frank.

In spite of these difficulties, the eight have other activities that help the time pass. Reading, of course, is a favorite. Lessons have begun, and Anne is studying English, Dutch, French, history, mathematics, and shorthand. She is interested as well in Greek and Roman mythology and art history. The women attend to the household chores, and the men do their share in maintaining security and making repairs. Each has one or more personal pastimes. Anne's hobby is collecting pictures of film stars and reading articles about the cinema. For Mr. Frank it is translating Dickens and reading classical German plays aloud to the group. All listen attentively to the short-wave radio, but now the large receiver downstairs has been turned over to the authorities on demand and has been replaced by an illegal "baby" set upstairs. News and other broadcasts are always material for extended discussions. The grown-ups recount stories of their youth. Riddles are asked all around. Some participate in practicing foreign languages. The women do needlework. A regular part of the routine is calisthenics since there is no opportunity for sports. Each person's birthday merits a celebration, usually highlighted by whatever delicacies of food, flowers, or other merchandise their protectors can procure on the market, where prices are soaring. Holidays, both Christian and Jewish, such as Hanukkah, St. Nicholas Day, Christmas, Whitsunday, and Easter are pleasant breaks in the monotony.

Despite their insular existence, the eight occupants of the secret apartment are not untouched by the events of the outside world. The war news affects one and all. They eagerly await their liberation in the form of an invasion by the Allies. The bombing of nearby German towns and air battles overhead keep them awake trembling with fear at night. The plight of the Jews sickens them, for cautious peeks through the curtains reveal trucks rolling along the streets filled with the persecuted on their way to concentration camps. Children in rags are begging in the streets, adult faces are grim. Many young Dutchmen are being sent to German labor camps. The Nazis play havoc with currency and ration books, causing even more consternation. Clothing that is outgrown or becomes too tattered is extremely difficult to replace. When one of their protectors becomes ill, a great handicap is created and the others must work overtime. Burglars frequently break into the warehouse below. Fortunately, the hidden rooms remain undiscovered.

Anne reflects on the conditions of life in the outside world. She is horrified at the grim aspect of Amsterdam life that she perceives in her occasional peeks through the curtains. Overcome by pity for the urchins begging in the streets, she wishes she might bring them upstairs for at least a good washing. Her conscience pricks her when she thinks of the relative safety and comfort of her existence compared to the wretched plight of the many Jews and others being sent to their deaths. Tales of the concentration camps and the atrocities committed by the Nazis before the inmates are gassed are so awful to Anne that she must force herself not to dwell on them. Reports of resistance measures taken by the Dutch people are encouraging at first but eventually depressing, for the Nazis quickly crush such actions and as punishment make conditions worse than before. How much she and the others despise the führer! Anne comments bitterly on the sort of German citizen created by Hitler and is thankful that although she was born a German she no longer qualifies as one since Hitler has denationalized all Jews. She eagerly awaits the day when she can acquire Dutch citizenship and vows to go to any length to achieve this goal, even if it means personally confronting Queen Wilhelmina. Despite the depressing awareness of the war outside their hiding place, Anne vows to keep up her spirits. She will force the dreadful thoughts out of her mind, for only in this way can she find a reason to believe in going on.

Looking inward, Anne often comments on how alone she feels. She realizes that she is set apart from the values and ideas of the grown-ups. She longs to be respected for her own opinions, rather then censured for what is considered juvenile impudence. She is also quite generous with her own criticisms of the others. She writes mournfully to Kitty of her alienation from her mother who, she feels, is not all a mother should be. Her father is her ideal but, in many ways, unreachable. Margot and she are too different in temperament and outlook to be close friends. She resents the preference of the others for her older sister. Peter lives in a shell and isn't that interesting. Mr. Dussel's slowness to understand things irritates Anne; his impatience with her is another sore point. Anne lacks respect for Mrs. van Daan's intelligence and finds her selfish and immodest. Anne feels herself the object of everyone's criticism. Each day she vows to overcome her faults, yet she is intent on remaining a distinct individual. Such conflicts are the subject of many letters to Kitty.

## JULY 11, 1943–AUGUST 1, 1944: THE SECOND YEAR

After a year together, the eight occupants are accustomed to the hazards both from within and from without. There are still the flare-ups between personalities, aggravated by the decreasing availability of supplies. The air raids are nerve-racking, and the war news affects their morale almost more than anything else. Illness visits each of the inhabitants by turn in the form of colds or flu. No medical help is available, so they must use home remedies and their limited supply of drugs. It is difficult to avoid contagion and impossible not to be an inconvenience to everyone else when illness strikes. Anne's eyes have grown so bad and her headaches so frequent and severe that the possibility of her going outside to an eye doctor is seriously considered, but the risk is too great. The weather causes more discomfort, particularly the summer heat because the windows must remain closed and curtained except at night. The desire to go outdoors frustrates everyone, particularly the younger ones. Keeping hope alive is a goal for each and all.

To make the passage of time more bearable for the young, Mr. Frank steps up the intellectual activity. For Margot there is a correspondence course in Latin, which she takes in Bep's name. Peter works harder at French. Anne and her sister are given some routine clerical work to do for the business. Anne's interest in genealogical tables is encouraged, and her father helps her work out the lineage of many European royal families.

As a precautionary measure, many pounds of dried peas and beans as well as tins of other foodstuffs were stored away before the group took up residence. Now some of the dried beans are spoiling, so there is a new project for everyone. Bean rubbing, to remove the mold that has formed on the bean skins, is an activity which aids the passage of time. Then, too, when the produce market is flooded with a certain commodity, the price is lowered and the occupants have that item purchased by their protectors in large quantities. When such amounts are delivered, all hands must set to work. Strawberries, for instance, must be prepared for jam, syrup, and canning whole. Similarly, shelling and preserving peas require a portion of everyone's time. But the novelty of such projects soon wanes, leaving everyone bored and somewhat sickened with peas and strawberries, which will have to be eaten nevertheless.

Food presents other problems, too. When ration shortages occur it is likely that only one or two foods will appear at all meals for several days or even weeks. Such items as lettuce, potatoes, kale, or spinach prepared in a variety of ways but served exclusively can result in disagreeable stomachs and dispositions. Table manners reflect the condition of current rations. Often conversations are simply extended wishful thoughts about which foods each person misses and longs for. As often as possible, Miep and Bep find some delicacy for the group, most often at holiday time or for someone's birthday.

Maintaining the physical security of the premises is of major importance, as burglars repeatedly break into the warehouse. Repairs must be made immediately, and the men are preoccupied with inspection and guard duty. Most fearsome are the air raids. Each occupant has prepared an "escape bag" in the event that an evacuation becomes necessary. But the problem in such a case is contradictory, for to leave the hideout would be as dangerous as remaining in a bombed building. Many discussions center around the better alternative, but no decision can be agreed on by all. Another pastime of the adults is political discussion after each radio broadcast. Often they are divided into two groups, the optimists and the pessimists. The discussions eventually lead to the same subject: Who will win the war? There is speculation about the war's outcome and the strategy of each country.

The most feverish item of debate is the forthcoming Allied invasion. When it occurs on June 6, 1944, hopes soar for a speedy liberation. But always they go back to questions of how soon and under what circumstances the war will end. Such discussions often become heated.

Other news of the outside reaches them from their protectors. The activities of the Dutch underground movement are of great interest. Although much information is encouraging, some incidents are cause for alarm. Their vegetable grocer is arrested for concealing Jews. Others involved in resistance are also punished by the Nazis. Anne is overcome with appreciation for the risks their own protectors take without voicing fear or complaints. The strain tells on their helpers. Mr. Kleiman has recurrent hemorrhages from a stomach ulcer and must be hospitalized. Bep's nerves are wearing thin from concerns over her sick father, her fiancé who has been sent to do forced labor in Germany, her office work, and her additional duties for the eight occupants. Miep and Jan have occasional illnesses that keep either one or both from helping their Jewish friends. Mr. Kugler receives a call-up to put in four weeks of forced labor. Then, too, one of the warehousemen displays curiosity about the upper floors. He must be carefully handled to curb his suspicions.

The second year is marked for Anne less by these events than by the alterations in her relationships with the others and those signs of her own mental and physical maturity. Looking back on her entries over the past year, she is rather surprised at some of the fury released on the pages. Although there are still personality conflicts among them all, Anne feels that she has learned to handle herself better and thus not cause criticism to be showered on her. Also, she recognizes that living in such confinement, compounded by the strain and tension of war, causes problems among people that might otherwise never occur. Therefore, she looks for good in others and tries to ignore the bad. Anne is aware that her relationship with her mother will never match the closeness between Margot and Mrs. Frank. Accepting this fact, she becomes more adept at not hurting her mother. Another outgrowth of her maturity is a new friendship with her sister. They can share much, but not everything. Anne also recognizes the ways she has grown away from her father and how, even from him, she has withheld parts of herself. These realizations increase her loneliness and feed her hunger for a friend. Her diary isn't the same as a real human being. Accompanying her longing for a companion with whom she can share mutual trust and understanding, she dreams intensely of her old friends, Lies Goslar and Peter Schiff.

One morning she awakes from a particularly vivid dream of Peter Schiff and that day seeks to initiate a friendship with Peter van Daan. Peter is shy and reserved, but Anne is persistent. Little by little, during the last half of the second year, the two form a relationship that develops from friendship into romance. Made aware of the dangers of unrestrained involvement by their parents, Anne and Peter control the relationship. They spend long hours together sharing confidences, ambitions, and fears. Vowing never to argue as they have seen their elders do, the girl, now fifteen, and the boy, just past seventeen, work out their problems in long, patient conversations. Anne soon realizes, however, that she is not in love with Peter, even though she has allowed him to give her the first kiss of her life. She is too aware of certain flaws in his character to commit herself to the thought of a future with him until she has seen how he grows up. She also realizes that although he has given her life an object when she needed it, Peter is more dependent on her than she on him. This is disconcerting, for Anne has discovered the need for self-reliance. She believes that with confidence and maturity, Peter will acquire this independence too, and perhaps she can help him toward this goal.

As important to Anne as her relationship with Peter is her relationship to herself. In this area the seeds of self-knowledge have been sown, and blossoming forth are a philosophy of life, a scale of values, a set of ideals, and a developing ambition for her future as an adult. Anne is aware of herself as an individual with values apart from those of her parents. Firm in her opinions, she contemplates her own behavior, that of the grown-ups, and the actions of humanity. Reflecting primarily on the conditions caused by the war, she remarks how cruel and futile war is. Fear and depression fostered by events outside and the confining conditions inside are combated by the lectures Anne gives herself to maintain courage, hope, and faith in God. Her spirits again revived, Anne considers her love of nature as a great source of consolation. Another uplifting thought is her newly realized ambition to be a journalist or a writer. In addition to the entries in her diary, she has written a few short stories. After the war she hopes to publish a book called *The Secret Annex*, using her diary as a guide.

Summarizing herself as "a bundle of contradictions," she discusses the lighthearted, seemingly superficial Anne that she displays to the world. In contrast, she writes of the deeper, finer Anne, who is too shy to reveal herself to the others. Questioning life's meaning, Anne explores the value of life versus death. Still searching, questioning, and answering, Anne makes a typical entry on Tuesday, August 1, 1944. Her diary ends there.

# COMMENTARY

## JUNE 12, 1942–JULY 8, 1942: LIFE ON THE OUTSIDE

### OUTLOOK

Because this is a diary, it is important to distinguish from the beginning those passages that tend to be more objective from those that are highly subjective. It is necessary also to be attuned to the moods of the writer, which, because of her age and circumstances, fluctuate greatly and are reflected by variations in tone throughout the diary. Because Anne is growing up, there are apt to be contradictions in her thinking. By the same token, some areas of her thinking develop consistently. One must remember too that the work itself was not initially intended as a finished product for publication. The diary was considered by Anne as a confidante, an imaginary friend to whom she could confess her most private thoughts and release her deepest emotions. There is no attempt by the author to control the content of her entries. In 1944 Anne learned on the radio that a Dutchman in exile in England hoped after the war to collect eyewitness accounts of Dutch suffering under the Germans. Anne determined to write a book based on her diary. Nevertheless, the diary reflects her impromptu and honest thoughts.

### A NEW FRIEND

The beginning of the diary is comprised of entries analogous to the beginning of any relationship. These include informative passages concerning Anne's background and present situation. It is as if she is introducing herself to Kitty with warmth but also with the natural reserve accorded a new friend. There is a note of cautious intimacy where Anne confides to Kitty her longing for the true friend she hopes the diary will prove to be. Remaining fairly objective in spite of due cause for bitterness, Anne describes the difficulties encountered by her family and others who are victims of

Hitler's anti-Jewish laws. Although the hardships and inconveniences make her wistful, she does not feel life to be unbearable. There are compensations, among them the attentions of her schoolmates. She rather boastfully describes her enjoyment of this popularity with a somewhat devil-may-care attitude. This is something Anne will look back on later, and in reflection it will be a signpost of her maturity.

**GROWN-UPS**

Anne's attitude toward the authority of grown-ups is revealed in this early section by her comments on her teachers. She is clever enough to amuse them even when she is being reprimanded. Because she can get off so lightly now, it is important to compare her later reactions to criticism and correction. Her independent spirit, even at this stage, is evident and should be interesting to trace through the diary.

**BOYFRIENDS**

It may seem at first peculiar that Anne has boyfriends. While these are not serious romantic relationships, they are not the same as friendships with girls. Rather, they are indications of her general popularity and feminine nature. Anne's only real crush is on Peter Schiff, but this again differs from a serious boy-girl attraction. It is another important item, because later on she will remember Peter and feel this early crush in a much more mature way. This is also an indicator of Anne's depth of feeling in its carryover from girlhood to young womanhood.

**ZIONISM**

Anne mentions that Hello Silberberg, one of her current admirers, secretly attends meetings of the Zionist movement, although his grandparents disapprove. Zionism was and still is a movement dedicated to the establishment of Palestine (now the state of Israel) as a homeland for the Jews. Hello's grandparents represent the Assimilationists, those opposed to Zionism on the grounds that it was more important for

Jews to become integrated citizens of the countries in which they resided despite overt anti-Semitism in Europe. Margot is interested in Zionism as indicated by her desire to be a teacher in Palestine after finishing school.

**PROGRESSIVE PARENTS**

Anne's mother and father might be considered modern with respect to their children's upbringing. They do not exert the traditional sort of disciplinary pressure on their daughters that might be expected from European parents. The Franks' philosophy later becomes a subject of controversy, and even Anne indicates an ambivalent attitude toward it. The earliest evidence of the Franks' progressive methods is the way they treat their daughters' grades at school. Rather than stress the importance of excellent report cards, the Franks feel that the girls should be happy, healthy, and polite, and the rest will take care of itself.

**SS CALL-UP**

The Franks have good cause for terror when Margot receives the call-up from the SS. It was not uncommon for the Nazis to take girls in their middle and late teens for the most unsavory purposes. Once a family member's name appeared on the call-up list, it was the end, not only for that particular individual but also for the entire family, whose doom was guaranteed. Despite any temporary success achieved in buying someone's name off a Nazi list, the eventual call-up came anyway. Therefore, the Franks were prudent in disappearing immediately after the first one came for Margot.

**DISAPPEARANCE**

Notice how the Franks have strived to preserve a normal existence until the last minute. Even their lodger, Mr. Goldschmidt, is not aware of changes in the household. It must not be thought that he and other uninvolved Dutch people were oblivious to the situation of the Jews. Many of those engaged neither in the underground movement nor the Dutch Nazi party simply looked away from all suspicious activities. To protect themselves, they remained neutral, and while deliberately knowing nothing could guess much. Theirs was not an enviable position, for they were suspected of knowledge by the Gestapo and distrusted as well by the underground. These uninvolved persons frequently suffered mistreatment from both sides.

## REACTION

Notice the different reactions of the members of the Frank family to the disappearance and first day in hiding. Because Anne is young it seems for her some sort of strange and romantic adventure. She is quite keyed up and eager to help her father with the work. Margot and Mrs. Frank are depressed and physically affected by the move. They are not able to cope with the chaos. But their adjustment into the new life comes more easily than Anne's once things are settled. It is not surprising that Mrs. Frank, accustomed to comfort and security, should be affected in this way. Perhaps Margot realizes less than her mother but more than her sister just what going into hiding means, and thus she reacts in a manner similar to that of Mrs. Frank. Mr. Frank seems able to cope with most of the circumstances as they arise. Like Anne, he has delayed reactions, but they naturally are less pronounced than those of his younger daughter, because of his maturity.

## STYLE

From the first entry in the diary, we are impressed by Anne's ability to organize and synthesize material. This is indicated by her orderly presentation of facts, lucid description of circumstances, and limited use of unnecessary adjectives. While she is organized and precise in her presentation, Anne does not overlook opportunities for personal comments and subtle indications of both her humorous and serious sides. Despite the tendency of young people to ramble on, once

Anne has discussed something she moves on to another topic with a surprising lack of awkwardness. Notice, too, the smooth insertions of dialogue that subtly indicate the personality of the speaker in a way compatible with Anne's descriptions of the person. This is important for subsequent character analysis, because it shows that although we see the characters from Anne's point of view, the revealing nature of the dialogue attests to the validity of her opinion.

## JUNE 12, 1942–JUNE 13, 1943: THE FIRST YEAR

### QUARRELS

It should come as no surprise that confinement and overexposure to one another cause personality conflicts among the first seven occupants. Mrs. Frank and Mrs. van Daan lose no time in developing a rivalry. It appears that their disagreements stem mainly from such trifles as communal dishes or linens, but one realizes that the two women have widely different standards and values. Mrs. Frank's social background is certainly higher than that of Mrs. van Daan. Hence, their personalities find deeper areas of conflict than those which appear on the surface over mundane matters. Even their methods of combat are different. Whereas Mrs. Frank usually withdraws after an arch remark with her cloak of dignity wrapped about her, Mrs. van Daan vents her emotions in a coarse barrage of angry words and frequent tears.

### THE FRANKS' FAMILY PROBLEMS

Anne's youth manifests itself in continuous chattering and seemingly impudent laughter. With all the pent-up energy of a thirteen-year-old and none of the physical outlets she formerly enjoyed, it is no wonder she annoys her elders. Consequently, their only recourse is to scold her or her parents. Margot is more unassuming than her younger sister and seems to annoy the others less, yet she too reacts, we are told by Anne, in the form of catty remarks and taking sides with her mother when Mrs. Frank and Anne have a flare-up. The relationship between Anne and her mother is strained because Anne obviously prefers her father. Realizing this, Mr. Frank is in an uncomfortable middle ground. He is wise enough to see Anne as passing through an Oedipal phase, not uncommon for young girls in which they are "in love" with their fathers and develop a rivalry with their mothers. Hence, Mr. Frank does his best to give Anne the affection she craves, combining it with a fatherly authority and encouragement to better behavior. Loyal to his wife and older daughter, he is the peacemaker of the family.

**THE VAN DAANS' FAMILY PROBLEMS**

The van Daans have their own family problems. As husband and wife, their relationship differs from that of Mr. and Mrs. Frank. Anne has never heard her parents quarrel, and she finds the van Daans' marital rows both upsetting and amusing. The van Daans seem to expend a good deal of energy in these quarrels, but Anne notes the tenderness with which they make up. Perhaps, she realizes, this is another kind of love between married people, and while different from that of her parents and not to her taste, it is love nevertheless. Peter, awkward and shy at this stage of his life, keeps pretty much to himself. Although the quarrels of his parents probably embarrass him, they are no novelty. This does not mean that he is immune to either the bickering or the confinements of life in hiding. At first he has symptoms of imaginary physical ailments; and his hypochondria is as valid a form of getting attention as Anne's chattering. Later we learn that Peter lets off steam by going up to the attic to swear. The only disciplinary incident in which he is notably involved concerns his clandestine reading of a forbidden book. Once again, it is Mr. Frank's duty as peacemaker to arbitrate between Mr. van Daan and his son.

**STRAIN OF CONFINEMENT**

It is not only the confinement that causes a strain on everyone's nerves. These two families are locked away from the civilization they have known. They have ceased to exist as far as the outside world is concerned. Their lives are in their own hands and those of their protectors. They have no function other than that of staying alive—and this at their own peril. They are helpless prisoners of time and fate. Surrounded by hostility from without, they have only one another to depend on and live for. All other concerns have been taken out of their lives. Marking time with no other function than continuing to live is a difficult exercise. Charged as they are with energy and emotion, it is small wonder that relationships are not worse. Living in constant fear of discovery, which means certain death, the seven must also cope with the immediacy of such a disaster. While everything that goes on in the outside world affects them, they are helpless to do anything about it. Their task is simply to endure and survive. Frustrated from within and without, these people have to cultivate what Mrs. Frank calls the "art of living." This means that seven individuals with distinct personal values and opinions must reorganize themselves into a different species of creature than they have ever imagined or experienced.

**THE DIARY AS AN OUTLET**

Anne retaliates for the reprimands she receives by "letting go" in her diary with comments that reveal fury, humor, and wisdom. At first, she writes a round of angry criticism aimed at whoever happened to annoy her. She even gloats if these individuals have been beaten in some other fray. Then she reflects on adult behavior in general, finding it far from flawless. She is perceptive enough to see that even though her elders have the advantage of age and can condemn her with relative impunity, their shortcomings are no more tolerable than her own. After she has released her anger, Anne pauses to consider herself. She attempts to rationalize the criticism she has received. As if holding up a mirror to herself she asks, "Am I really so bad?" After a few more blusters, she vows to outgrow her failings and to set such a good example that all will be forever silent in awe of her perfection. As she gradually cools off, Anne makes some humorous worldly-wise remark signifying that she is ready to sally forth again now that self-repairs have been made.

**DAILY LIFE**

Some of Anne's best descriptions are those concerning the little aspects of everyday living that a less observant person might overlook. The facts of life and nature's necessities are treated by Anne with surprising maturity and honesty. She manages to give even the greatest inconveniences caused by faulty plumbing or indigestible food a touch of humor. Anne's curiosity and wholesomeness enable her to take a lesson about the external sex differences of cats from Peter van Daan without batting an eye. Of course, Peter's open attitude is extremely helpful. Anne realizes here that some of her schoolyard whispers on such topics were ridiculous.

**OTHER JEWS**

Anne recounts to Kitty the gloomy stories of Jews being deported and sent from Holland to German concentration camps. She feels guilty for her own safe existence. It is almost more than she can bear when she thinks of her young friends being mistreated and killed. But this is one of the realities of war with which all must cope. Her parents, too, know of their friends' deportations and deaths. Their protectors try to keep such news from the Franks and van Daans, but the radio is not choosy about its listeners. Anne is incredulous at the cruelty of the Gestapo and the innocence of their victims. Such periods of contemplation often result in hopeless tears followed by little pep talks in which she revives her courage and her faith. But there is no answer to why all this must be.

**INTELLECTUAL ACTIVITY**

Notice how eager Anne is for intellectual activity. This is not only the result of being deprived of other forms of amusement. Her wide range of serious interests is an indicator of her intellectual curiosity. The reports in her diary of translating books from other languages show her verbal proficiency. She dislikes all forms of mathematics but does not seem unable or unwilling to do her assignments. Mr. Frank is a great source of intellectual stimulation for Anne. Realizing the needs of his daughter's keen mind, he seeks ways for her to exercise her mental power, giving much of his own time to partake in these endeavors with her. Often Anne remarks that as soon as the war is over she can return to school, but she seems to be doing an excellent job of keeping up on her own in the meantime.

**RATIONING**

During the war there was a worldwide shortage of consumer products. This was caused by the diversion of raw materials into war goods, and by the impossibility of transporting materials through customary land, sea, and air channels. As supplies were limited, governments (including that of the United States) issued to their citizens ration books containing coupons for different types of commodities. These included food and any article made from materials being converted to war use, such as rubber, nylon, petroleum, and leather. Ration books were intended to limit the quantity of available supplies and to provide equal distribution among the populace. It was possible in some instances to get extra ration books illegally. (The Franks had four illegal books.) It was also possible, but costly, to procure rationed articles on the black market.

**HOLIDAYS**

Most readers are familiar with the Christian holidays Christmas and Easter and the Jewish holiday Hanukkah. Less familiar, probably because they are not as widely celebrated in the United States, are Whitsunday and St. Nicholas Day. The seventh Sunday after Easter is known as Whitsunday, commemorating the descent of the Holy Ghost. Another religious idea connected with Whitsunday is that on this day the apostles were filled with wisdom (wit) by the Holy Ghost. St. Nicholas Day occurs on December 6 and commemorates this popular saint who has become the patron saint of Russia, Aberdeen (Scotland), scholars, pawnbrokers, little boys, and parish clerks. He is also the original figure on whom Santa Claus is based. Although the occupants of the hiding place are Jewish, they celebrate these Christian holidays to relieve the tedium. Yet they show as much respect for these unaccustomed Christian festivals as for their own Jewish holidays.

## JEWISH IDENTITY

Anne's sense of being Jewish has its ups and downs. Made aware of her religion from an early age, she has felt less piety than awareness of belonging to a separate group. She reflects much on the Jews versus the Germans, stating with precocious insight that the two groups are the "greatest enemies in the world." Behind Anne's sense of identity is a historical pattern of anti-Semitism and Jewish segregation in Europe. Even the wealthy, cultured, upper-middle-class Jews from which Anne's family comes have not been immune to prejudicial treatment. Those Jews permitted educational and social privileges were never fully accepted into the societies in which they lived. The history of the Jews is one of group living tightly contained for protection against anti-Semitism. Anne is part of this traditional pattern of European Jewry. Therefore, she is able to accept with a surprising degree of tolerance the initial anti-Semitic legislation and the early hardships. Her comments regarding the progressively harsher treatment of the Jews reflect more horror and pity than bitterness, more outrage against persecution in general. Then, too, from her protected though risky position in hiding, she has lost the fullest sense of identification. Thus set apart, she can view with objectivity the plight of the Jews, and while she might feel guilty about her safety and comfort, she is less apt to feel the extremes of personal bitterness that more direct contact would have created. Anne must be understood as: (1) inherently aware of her separate identity as a Jew; (2) victimized by Hitler's persecution of the Jews; and (3) a temporary bystander whose suspended participation enables her to view things with more objective sympathy.

Contrast Anne's Jewish identification with that of Peter or Margot. Peter is decidedly bitter and resentful about being a Jew. He contemplates converting to Christianity after the war. Anne finds this a distressing idea and tries to convince him that he will always be a Jew because of his birth, and if he comes through the trials of Hitler's persecution, there will be no need to convert anyway. Margot, on the other hand, strongly identifies with her Jewish heritage, and it seems reasonable to assume that she has Zionist leanings. Although secretive about her plans for the future, she indicates a desire to teach or do other work in Palestine. Anne tends to be more of an Assimilationist. Intent on retaining her identity as a Jew, she would nevertheless like to become a Dutch citizen after the war.

**POLITICS**

Although much of Anne's political opinion is formed by the attitude of the grown-ups, she is independent enough in her thinking and expression to comment astutely and with sophisticated humor on many public personalities and war developments. Notice her utter contempt and disgust for Hitler and her ability to see through his propaganda. Many of her remarks indicate a wisdom beyond her years. For instance, when the others are selfishly impatient for the Allied invasion to begin, Anne explains in her diary how much more important it is for the English to defend their own territory and employ aggression on other battlefronts despite the anxiety of the Dutch under German occupation. How needlessly, according to Anne, the grown-ups frustrate one another with constant speculation and debate over political affairs. She realizes, too, how important these events are to their welfare, not only in terms of ultimate liberation but also for providing conversational material, even if the result is a quarrel. Notice the familiarity with which she speaks of Winston Churchill, Dwight D. Eisenhower, and other leaders in the War.

**EFFECTS OF WAR**

Consider the stamina of these people under the strain of confined quarters, short rations, the threat of discovery—all compounded by the nerve-racking air raids. The bombing of nearby German towns can be plainly heard. Nazi antiaircraft guns based in Holland open fire regularly. Air battles take place overhead between the Allies and Nazis, creating the possibility of unintended disaster for the Dutch below. No wonder Anne and the others react with trembling, tears, upset stomachs, and short tempers. All they can do is hope and pray that their building will not be hit. Their "escape bags," as Anne pointed out, are just psychological devices for the sake of having something to hold on to. Only too well do they know that leaving their hideout would be as lethal as having a bomb come through the roof. Mrs. van Daan's hysterics are a source of amusement and pity for Anne, depending on how badly she herself is affected. Notice Anne's continual attempts to be stoical under such circumstances and how annoyed with herself she becomes when she reacts with uncontrollable fear. Many seasoned soldiers returned from the war with symptoms of shell shock from just such conditions as those experienced by the eight in hiding. It is noteworthy, then, how really strong these people were in resisting severe nervous disorders from knowledge of their defenselessness.

**GROWING PAINS**

As the first year in hiding draws to an end, we can look back on Anne's entries in her diary and see significant areas of maturation. Not unique among persons her age are the "growing pains" that signify the end of childhood and the beginning of adulthood. This uncomfortable period of adolescence is familiar to contemporary readers. At the time of Anne's writing the subject of adolescent problems was not as highly publicized as it is now. Nor were Europeans as predisposed to talking about such topics as Americans. The traditional European attitude toward young people is reflected in the comments of Dussel and the van Daans, who find the flexibility of the Franks with respect to their daughters' upbringing rather shocking and too modern. The Franks seem more progressive and more like American parents in their broad-mindedness and permissiveness. Anne resents in some ways her parents' methods, often feeling that she lives in a deserted world, one that lacks concrete, traditional authority. Probably Anne would have resented far more the traditional authoritarian upbringing expounded by Dussel. No doubt, under either system, the sensitive girl would have suffered the same "growing pains," but with different results.

**ISOLATION**

Anne never writes of being punished, although she complains of being criticized, reprimanded, and lectured. When she has behaved poorly, she might be ignored by the others for a day or so, but her parents do not practice such overt methods of punishment as the van Daans, who send Peter to his room without supper in one instance. The means by which Anne is disciplined are subtler. Moreover, as a perceptive person, she is able to sense the understated methods and to take on part of the burden of her own punishment and upbringing. This explains many of the lectures she gives herself in her diary. These entries are examples of her process of reasoning through her behavior and coming to terms with herself independently of external authority.

**RESPONSIBILITY**

The awareness of being responsible to and for her own actions is the basic cause of Anne's sense of isolation. Responsibility is a lonely thing, for it eliminates the dependence on others with whom to share the blame or the praises that result from actions taken. That is why Anne so often writes to Kitty that she feels alone, without good advice or good examples. Having passed out of childhood, she realizes that she no longer qualifies for the amount of spoiling and protection children are permitted. Neither does she inherit the approval and acceptance of an adult. Confused by this status, she is apt to laugh or cry when neither reaction is desired, but either may occur from the emotional excess within her. She realizes that only through her own efforts will she conquer her shortcomings.

**LONELINESS**

Other factors contribute to Anne's sense of isolation. There is the simple fact that among the inhabitants of the hideout there is no one with whom Anne can establish a friendship of the sort she enjoyed on the outside. People tend to be selective in forming friendships, usually on the basis of similar interests, experiences, and age. Other than Peter, who is shy and at first does not appeal to Anne, there is no one in the group who fits the pattern Anne followed in making friends before going into hiding. Family relationships usually exist on a level different from that of friendship among peers, although as children reach maturity, they often discover a solid friendship on an adult level with a brother, sister, or parent. But this does not usually occur until adulthood. Outside Anne's family group the rest are strangers with whom she has a living arrangement and nothing more. She may discover areas of fondness for certain individuals among them, but the initial artificiality of their living in such close circumstances under duress does not provide a natural background for the formation of friendships. Thus Anne must rely on her imagination either to summon up the memory of her former friends from school or to create a mythical friend such as Kitty, her diary. Anne is resourceful enough to do both of these things, but her loneliness grows even more from the natural fact that communication is a two-way process, and with imaginary friends one lives, in effect, alone.

## DEVELOPMENT OF STYLE

How has Anne's writing developed during the first year? It is likely that until now she has had neither the opportunity nor the necessity to write so extensively. With practice, one's skill is bound to improve, but since this is a private endeavor, there is no one to correct or comment on her writing. But there are other means by which Anne's skill may grow, and although less effective than correction by an authority, her writing is bound to improve. First of all, Anne reads a great deal. The books are for the most part by accomplished writers. They have a subconscious effect on her own writing. The few flourishes that occur as breaks in her otherwise straightforward style are the results of her attempts to imitate the professional techniques of other writers. There are also passages in which one can detect the refinements in her own style. These occur in certain ways, such as the foreshortening of a descriptive passage into crisper, more pungent sentences lacking connectives. Another example is her developing sense of metaphor, by which suggestion replaces long-windedness. Last, her sentence structure is becoming more complex.

## MATURITY OF CONTENT

Her content is marked by a surprising objectivity, despite the personal nature of a diary. She steps outside herself and sees the character of Anne Frank at a distance, despite the use of the first-person pronoun. Her comments on the others in the group are also gaining in objectivity as she matures. Notice how she begins to rationalize their behavior rather than simply criticize it. Notice, too, that her criticism usually has much validity and is not simply an outburst of petty complaints. On the other hand, we cannot fail to suspect

Anne of selecting the most dramatic instances for illumination. This, however, bespeaks her selectivity as a writer.

## JULY 11, 1943–AUGUST 1, 1944: THE SECOND YEAR

### THE ART OF LIVING

The first entry of the second year in hiding calls attention to the fact that Anne has matured in a particular aspect of the "art of living." She refers to her new practice of "hypocrisy" when dealing with other people instead of letting fly some plain talk as she did in the past. This is a sophisticated attitude. Anne has realized that getting on with others often requires deference to someone else's ego and disregarding one's own. She has found that if she pretends to accept a situation or a remark, an argument will be avoided. This method of avoiding strife is still a somewhat new exercise in self-control, and Anne remarks that she often forgets her part in the little performance. Voicing opposition to an injustice without remembering what she has taught herself often results in strife. It is obvious that she is not especially content in this new knowledge, feeling that if she is in the right, she can be honest only by expressing herself.

### STOOPING TO CONQUER

The incident between Anne and Dussel over the use of the table in the room they share is a good revelation of character as well as good example of Anne's competence as a writer. Dussel exemplifies the typical Old World attitude toward children. His behavior in this matter is less an example of bad manners than a way of thinking about young people. Notice the way he minimizes Anne's need for the use of the table by making trifles of her work projects. To his way of thinking, no child of fourteen could be engaged in serious work. What probably enrages Dussel all the more is Anne's mention of her rights. This notion is out of the question as far as Dussel is concerned, for "rights" have the connotation of dealings between equals. To Dussell, a child does not have equal claim to privileges. Also noticeable are elements of Dussel's peevishness and Anne's capacity for getting around people. The incident is proof of the girl's new method of diplomacy. She allows Dussel to think he has won the match before she takes final action and with the help of her father gains the use of the table without causing a major clash within the group.

## HUMOR AND JUSTICE

Regarding style, we notice the humorous overtones with which Anne has described an incident of combat in which she was involved. Without the aid of her sense of humor, the account could have become a petty, unpleasant attempt at self-justification and simply an outlet for her fury. Instead, the writer has drawn an incident between two characters with the objectivity of an observer. Read without the first-person pronoun, the incident might easily pass for the work of an author using fictional characters for the purpose of illustrating the theme of justice. It should be evident to all by now that justice is a subject with which Anne is both intellectually and personally involved. Her illustrations of the topic are well noted for their pungency as well as depth of exploration.

## PRECOCIOUS CHILD'S THREAT

Seen from the point of view of Mrs. van Daan or Dussel, a youngster with Anne's perception and intelligence is far from a pleasure. To someone like Mrs. van Daan, whose intelligence is average, a child such as Anne can pose a threat, for with added years and experience the youngster will outstrip her elders and assume a superior position. It is to her advantage to keep Anne in her place. Mr. Dussel, while not intellectually threatened by the girl, finds Anne a nuisance mainly because his life does not include much contact with children (he has none of his own) and because he finds fault with her upbringing. In the latter sense, he finds his position as an adult threatened. Allied in their respective weaknesses, Mr. Dussel and Mrs. van Daan lose no opportunity to enhance their positions by finding fault with Anne. The procedure stems from an instinct of self-protection. In contrast Mr. Frank's handling of his daughter is more positive, although many parents also feel threatened by exceptional children.

## A TYPICAL DAY

Anne gives a full account of a typical day in the hiding place. Even here she is able to inject humor and a personal tone quite sophisticated for a fourteen-year-old. Observant of the little mannerisms each person displays, she makes the timetable seem alive with personalities rather than a mere tally sheet of dull routine. Considering the trying limitations of their activity, it seems astonishing that so much can be written about so pitifully little. But Anne, with the ability to observe more than surface action, creates an atmosphere of throbbing life filled to the brim with purposeful incident. Included in Anne's timetable is a critique of each character at the evening meal. This commentary resembles the anecdotes under photographs of students in a yearbook: witty, concise, and revealing. Notice in this passage the mention of their protectors. Miep and Jan, Bep, Kleiman, and Kugler function as more than sympathizers with a job to do. The helpers are almost members of the hideout, for they share the meals, the conversation, and the danger. Having thus sealed their fate with the inhabitants, they are considered full-fledged members of the little community. Despite the strain on personalities, each person, occupant or protector, has achieved a vital function in the underground corporation.

## FEAR AND STILLNESS

Anne mentions over and over the two things that disturb her the most—the fear and the stillness. These are the enemies with which she cannot cope as successfully as she can with interpersonal problems. The stillness to which Anne refers is especially oppressive on Sundays. This is mainly because there is no business activity downtown where they live, and because of the war, very few people spend the day strolling along the streets. If anyone is to be seen through the slit in the curtains, it is usually someone in a great hurry to reach a destination. Grim-faced and war-weary, the once-bustling populace now keeps to its shelters. With nothing to do and no people to hear or watch engaged in the weekday routine, Anne finds the stillness terrifying, almost like that of a deserted world. This atmosphere gives rise to thoughts that the usual amount of activity can keep away. It promotes reflection and brings to mind those horrors of war that Anne must continually fight in order to avoid despair. Reading and sleep are the only methods of combating the stillness and the fear it brings. She feels at these times even more alienated from those with whom she shares the life in hiding.

**NEW IDEAS**

Once again, Mr. Frank comes to the aid of his daughters, whose intellectual appetites are never satisfied. For Margot, he has arranged a correspondence course in Latin, which she will take in Bep's name. For Anne he has selected the New Testament—a subject that seems incompatible with the Franks' religious beliefs. Margot feels uncomfortable about the thought of such a book as a Hanukkah gift for Anne. Mr. Frank agrees, and it is decided that the gift will be for St. Nicholas Day. Consider for a moment the motives behind a Jewish father giving his daughter the New Testament. It appears that Mr. Frank is a broad-minded man whose intellect far exceeds his prejudices. It is compatible, too, with the modern methods by which he is raising his daughters; Mr. Frank wants Anne to be exposed to the fundamental ideas on which her civilization is based. Perhaps, too, he feels that the philosophy of Jesus may lift Anne's spirits, and that the content of the New Testament will help her to understand her own religion better. By opening up such a broad area of thought to his daughter, Mr. Frank may have provided Anne with endless hours of intellectual occupation. Comparing the selection of new studies for Anne and Margot, one can detect the differences in each girl's mental preferences and capabilities. Anne considers Margot her intellectual superior, but the older girl tends to prefer the narrower, more disciplined aspects of study, while Anne seeks the broader, more interpretive ones. Both girls are obviously quite intelligent; Anne's feeling of inferiority to Margot is probably the result of their differences in age and personality.

**IMAGINATION**

The quality of Anne's imagination is evident in all her entries, but particularly so when she tries to relate her past, present, and future existence to a larger system of being that will unify the three. She finds it difficult to conceive that she was ever the girl who lived among other people, went to school, had friends, enjoyed sports, and had a big roomy house occupied by only one family. That seems to be a different person. Contemplating a mode of life after the war is also difficult. She knows that much physical destruction has taken place, and that the facilities of life will be greatly changed. But the precocious girl is equally aware of the spiritual and psychological changes that have occurred in the people, both those with whom she lives and those on the outside. More brutal than these intuitions is the knowledge that many of the people she has known are dead. From these thoughts Anne develops a beautiful metaphor of her isolation that approaches allegory in its attempt to make concrete all that she finds so unreal.

**GHASTLY PROPHECY**

In describing the accident that befell her fountain pen, Anne endows her lost possession with a personality of its own. The fate of the fountain pen gives rise to a chilling prophecy that Anne makes unintentionally. The pen has been cremated, and that is the fate Anne wishes for herself after death, not knowing that that is exactly what is happening to millions of Jews.

**DREAMS AND GUILT**

Weighing even more heavily on Anne's mind is her former schoolfriend, Hanneli (Lies) Goslar. The entry in the diary concerning Anne's vision of her friend is heartrending—almost prayerful. How desperately Anne reaches out for Hanneli through mists of memory leading into remorse. One wonders just what insignificant act of girlish jealousy occurred that causes Anne to feel so guilty. More likely it is guilt of another kind that brings to Anne's memory the minor incident of rivalry over a new friendship Hanneli had made. The guilt Anne feels is understandable. She and her family are safe from the Nazis in the little world they have created for themselves. In spite of the difficulties of their everyday lives, there is no comparison to the horrors and privations that have befallen Hanneli and her family. It is as if Anne wishes to repent for her own well-being, and Hanneli is an identifiable symbol through whom Anne can reach the unknown thousands of persecuted people in sympathy and regret. The haunting image of Hanneli is indicative of that "deeper, finer" side that Anne feels too shy to reveal to anyone but Kitty.

**FEMININE MODESTY**

When Anne is ill with the flu, many home remedies are applied, and Dussel, who has had medical training, feels it is his responsibility to give the sick girl professional attention. Notice Anne's revulsion toward his contact with her body. This is indicative of more than just the shyness of a young girl whose sense of her physical maturity is confusing. Anne's attitude reveals an awareness of developing sensuality, the earliest longings of womanhood. She is resentful of physical contact with Dussel because he is not the appropriate image of her young fancy. She has too many other associations with Dussel, and the nearness of the older man embarrasses and upsets her because of their established relationship. Like so many girls undergoing similar phases of development, Anne rejects the very longing itself because it is unfamiliar, and when stimulated by unsuitable and unexpected incidents, her reaction is naturally one of disgust and rejection. Before or after this awkward phase, Dussel's medical attention would pass unnoticed. Considering Dussel's attitude toward Anne, it is even less likely that there is anything improper about his examining or treating her. Later Anne reads a book that explains this awkward and exaggerated physical modesty.

**CONFINEMENT**

How painful it must be for Anne to hear of Kleiman's daughter, Jopie, and her active life in the outside world. Anne must remind herself that if Jopie is fortunate in comparison to her, she is fortunate in comparison to other Jewish children not hidden away from the persecutors. Anne's longing for fun and freedom is another of the great tortures she is teaching herself to endure. She admits that when strong substitutional thinking fails, her only relief is tears. One marvels further at the absence of bitterness or cynicism in Anne's overall thinking.

**NEW FAMILY ATTITUDES**

Reading through the pages of Anne's diary we notice the changes of her attitude toward her father. Now, just past midway, it becomes evident that there is a development in her feelings about Pim that indicates her development from a little girl into a woman. Mr. Frank was right a year and a half before in saying that Anne would outgrow her "Oedipal" crush on her father. No longer one of childish hero worship, nor the uncomfortable possessiveness toward an imaginary lover, Anne's concept of her father has become mature in that he exists as an equal insofar as his human suffering and experiences are concerned. Of course he is still held in the exalted position of Father, but this is now tempered by Anne's own experiences of pain and longing, of trial and triumph. Now he can confide in his younger daughter those things with which he would trust an adult. Out of their former closeness has grown a special friendship not uncommon among members of a family who are similar in nature and spirit. Anne has worked very hard to gain this friendship and confidence, often overextending herself and at times withdrawing. Mr. Frank has stood by watching his daughter mature, always holding his feeling for her within the bounds of discretion so that his wife and other daughter had their fair share of his affections. Now, if there is favoritism, it is not of the destructive kind that can occur in families but the natural preference of kindred souls. Anne feels with well-grounded confidence that those special interchanges of thought between her and her father do not extend to the other members of the family despite his genuine affection for them.

**SUFFERING**

What should also be evident is that Anne's concept of suffering has broadened beyond the self-centered sort in which she at first indulged. True, she felt remotely the sense of suffering experienced by those in the outside world—especially those she had known. But what has occurred is an ability both to sympathize and identify with the pain of others. This comes from a variety of painful experiences coupled with the ability to see beyond the pain and to relate the individual experience to that of others in ever-widening circles until all humanity is encompassed. This concept does not come equally to those who mature chronologically. Many adults do not identify with the pain of others to a great extent, although they may give lip service to others' suffering. Mrs. van Daan, for example, is an adult who reacts to pain in this limited way. In contrast, Mr. Frank's experiences of pain, although kept to himself for the most part, generate a sympathy for humankind. Anne is in the process of developing this quality, which is as intense as poetry and as deep as philosophy. Notice how she is moved in her writing to both poetic and philosophical expression. Notice, too, her understanding of painful experience as the source of her father's tolerance, and her hope that she may learn from his example.

**NEW YEAR'S REFLECTIONS**

Looking back on the entries in her diary, Anne notes the outbursts of fury against her mother which, at this point, seem quite shocking and cause her pangs of conscience. Wishing to clarify the record and to indicate her present understanding of why those entries were so unattractively one-sided, Anne reflects on her behavior and attitude. She first discusses the reasons for having written so tempestuously, realizing that many of these outbursts were the outlets for moods now dealt with differently. She recognizes the ways she has matured, so that she no longer has such a one-sided view of people, her mother in particular. In a calm and adult manner, Anne accepts the facts that (1) she and her mother do not basically understand each other and may never do so, even though they can get along by exercising patience and restraint, and (2) her love for her mother is not of the customary dependent sort experienced in similar relationships. Her search for the reason behind the conflicts with her mother culminates temporarily in her realization that Mrs. Frank desires to be friends with her daughters rather than a typical parent. This explains the gaping need Anne has for maternal authority. Anne has had to find in her imagination her image of what a mother should be. Much of what Anne feels is valid and understandable, but the problem works both ways. No doubt Mrs. Frank feels equally alienated from a precocious daughter who favors her father. For a person as sensitive as Anne, the experience of growing up is so difficult that Mrs. Frank has stepped aside, realizing that she cannot cope with the situation. In time, it seems inevitable for Anne to understand and accept her mother as an individual and fret less about the ideal parent she imagines.

## DREAMS OF THE PAST

From out of Anne's short past comes the image of Peter Schiff in a dream so real that Anne has the sensation of his touch upon her cheek. Recalling that of all her boyfriends from former days, Peter Schiff was the one she secretly cared for, the reader should have no trouble understanding how Anne's present state of loneliness could cause her to invoke his memory so powerfully. In a similarly vivid way, Anne has dreamt of Hanneli and both grandmothers. Such dreams indicate the sense of closeness Anne has felt for these people but has never been able to communicate fully. Therefore, in dreams, she goes back to individuals from her past, fulfilling in this capacity the incomplete relationships. These dreams are motivated by her extreme loneliness and intense desire to be close to someone. Notice how the release of these emotions by the dream process affects Anne and how much better she feels physically and mentally.

## A LOVE OBJECT

Another important aspect of Anne's dream of Peter Schiff is her developing sexual maturity. Convinced that she has always understood "the longing," at least in her mind, Anne is now beginning to experience it physically. Having discussed such matters with her parents, more so with her father, Anne has also read a book for young girls on the topic. Although she understands much in theory, the reality of physical desire developing within her body fascinates and delights her. Again we see how Anne is able to take an objective view of her inmost self. The result of this process of maturity causes in Anne an even more desperate need for a love object. Because of this need, her fantasy of Peter becomes more understandable. Note Anne's sense of propriety and restraint where matters of physical affection are concerned. She may feel her love for the boy of her past to be complete, but she is not permissive, even in fantasy. He may touch only her face. For Anne, the dream of Peter signals a new phase in her life. It changes her attitudes to relationships with others and affects her feelings about herself. The need for a love object has been satisfied at least in fantasy by Peter. A sense of fulfillment has given Anne a different perspective now that she has found an object for her emotions. Yet imaginary companionship is not satisfying. What develops emotionally for Anne henceforth will be more understandable in terms of this notion.

**LOVE TRANSFER**

Just after Anne's dream of Peter Schiff, she finds herself suddenly interested in getting to know Peter van Daan, whom she has virtually ignored for the past year and a half. While she seems to be surprised at her newly found interest in him, it really is a natural outgrowth of the dream. In more specialized terminology, Anne's interest in Peter van Daan would be called a "transference." This means that love is transferred from one object to another, seeking with each change the satisfaction unattainable with the previous one. With Anne, the pattern is basic and natural. The primary image, of course, is an ideal figure. At first it is her father. Maturing both intellectually and emotionally, she realizes that her father is not "the one." The second ideal figure is Peter Schiff. But again, the transfer has been from one unattainable object to another. The next object is Peter van Daan. He is real and attainable, and Anne transfers the ideal image to him along with her affections. It will be interesting to see how she discovers that the ideal of love must be tempered by the faults and imperfections of the love object.

**ANNE AND PETER**

At first Anne suffers the pangs of uncertainty that every new relationship between members of the opposite sex entails. The flirtation, withdrawal, anxiety, and infatuation fill the moments of Anne's new world. Little by little she becomes less afraid of being a nuisance to Peter, and he gradually overcomes his shyness. Anne senses behind his awkwardness and former habit of solitude a longing as deep as hers for companionship. She skillfully draws him out of his shell, at the same time delighting in the new meaning he has given her life. He has provided her with the security she craved, and now this confidence in his affection in enables her to be less defensive with the other occupants. Her relationships with all of them improve, most noticeably with her mother, sister, and Mrs. van Daan. This is because she has found her identity as a woman in the relationship with Peter. Maintaining discretion and restraint in their physical affection is important to both young people, and Mr. Frank's heart-to-heart talk with each one separately helps them to understand how important self-control is in their confining circumstances. Nevertheless, the mild aspects of physical love are for both Anne and Peter important as marks of maturity. In Anne's commentary one can detect her objective interest in the subject, again displaying a mature and perceptive attitude. While the grown-ups are pleased that Anne and Peter have found each other, they take a dim view of the possible consequences of too strong an attachment. Despite the teasing and stern remarks made by the adults, the two young people manage quite well to conduct their relationship on a satisfying and wholesome level.

## REALISM

After Anne's relationship with Peter van Daan, the second most important aspect of her maturity this second year is her developing sense of realism. Because she is basically an idealist, Anne has suffered greatly from the realities of life. This is not to say that Anne has lost her ideals—far from it. But what has occurred is a tempering of them with experiences and deep thinking that have combined to teach her that although one has the right to expect much, one must be grateful for even a fraction of what was expected. In connection with this, Anne has learned to expect as much from herself as from others. A problem growing out of the sense of self-reliance is a little overdose of independence, which disturbs her parents, particularly her father, whom she hurts at one point, though she is then forgiven. Anne derives new strength and conviction from her realistic attitude. For one so young, it may seem rather frightening that Anne now sees each moment of life in the here and now as holding more importance than the vague, distant future. It may seem an almost cynical attitude, until one considers the effects of the war and the threat of death, which have been, perhaps, the most forceful influences in shaping Anne's realism. This is basically a form of protection against intense suffering. Grief cannot be tolerated by most people in large quantities, and very sensitive individuals are most prone to emotional disorders when they cannot cope with mental and spiritual anguish. Through tireless effort, Anne has learned to cope with her suffering by thinking things through to a suitable conclusion. Accepting the brutalities of the present was probably for her the most difficult task, for her imagination was enabled to escape by projecting back into the past or forward into the future. However, as the past became more remote and the future more uncertain, Anne had to accept the present, and then it was all meaningful. In strengthening her sense of reality, she has also done much to reinforce her ideals by making them conform to a more practical pattern. That is, she has learned to accept the possibility that every person and situation may fall short of perfection, but tat she can still seek it in striving to improve herself and giving aid to others. One does not usually come to this wisdom at such an early age.

**SELF-OBSERVER**

Reflecting on the girl she used to be, Anne has cataloged her own development with wisdom, emotion, objectivity, and honesty. She has experienced all the phases of maturity to date as both participant and observer. Her accomplishments are commendable, for she has undertaken to be responsible for her own growing up. She has developed a concept of life that strives for perfection but does not deny imperfection. Although she still has her moments of doubt and rejection, of fear and uncertainty, Anne's overall outlook is positive. It is manifested as the diary progresses by improvements in her relationships with others. If she cannot accept them totally, she can at least understand why not and then find a rapport with each one based on the qualities she finds acceptable. She endeavors to see the best in people and to bring out the best in herself even when it would be easier to give in to selfishness and self-interest. Anne is able to care for those people in whom she finds weakness and to be truthful about her emotions. For example, she knows that she is not seriously in love with Peter van Daan but finds value in the affection they feel for each other. She realizes that he is more dependent on her than she on him but feels she can help him as he has helped her. She is disappointed about his weaknesses but does not close her mind to the possibility that he might improve. Anne has also come to terms with her parents and her sister, appreciating them for what they are instead of despising them for not being what she selfishly wishes them to be. She has cultivated a realistic sense of the future and the possibility that it might not come about. She has acquired goals that are valuable for the present even if they can never be realized.

## LASTING PHILOSOPHY

Events move along swiftly toward the end of the second year. The Allied invasion of Normandy has occurred, and all anticipate the liberation of Holland. Now Anne's political commentary is more opinionated and more frequent. The end of their confinement seems near. The war tells on the inhabitants. Mrs. van Daan is very near hysteria. All are impatient, frightened, hopeful. Anne has been accepted as an equal by the younger generation of the hideout, who have formed a faction with rather definite ideas that differ from those of the grown-ups. The young people have found a sense of group identity and no longer function as selfish and competitive individuals to the degree that they did previously. Anne has gone up in the estimation of Peter and Margot and is rather surprised at their compliments. While there are still quarrels among them all, they do not seem to disturb Anne as severely.

The last few entries summarize Anne's philosophy. She is aware that she has matured, perhaps beyond her years. Still introspective, she is capable of self-reproach and depression. But her overall attitude is one of optimism—a belief so forceful that she is certain it can sustain her no matter what happens. It is curious that the last entry is so melancholy with self-inquiry. One turns the page expecting a new note of optimism the next day. But there is nothing more. The end of the book comes as unexpectedly as the end of safety came to the eight occupants. Yet it is not the end, for in the world's memory, Anne Frank lives on.

# CHARACTER ANALYSES

## NOTE

It has been said that the characters in *The Diary of a Young Girl* are one-dimensional because they are presented from only one point of view. Although this is technically true, it takes no account of the reader's responsibility to investigate the other angles of vision made possible in subtle ways. Aside from what Anne tells us about the other seven members of the group, their actions as well as their remarks permit us to make our own inferences regarding their characters. Another aspect in the reader's favor is the limited background. With a broader range of setting in which to disguise many facets of their personalities, the eight major characters might never reveal their personality traits as they do within the confines of their hiding place. In such a case, we would be forced to accept the author's point of view. The limited setting aids the reader in making his or her own decisions regarding aspects of personality the author's youth and mood might have caused her to overlook. It is interesting to contrast the author's description of character with the reader's perception and to determine the comparative validity of each.

## MAJOR CHARACTERS

### ANNE

Introduced by herself as a thirteen-year-old German-Jewish girl living in Holland with her parents and sister to avoid Nazi persecution, Anne states that the purpose of her diary is to unburden her innermost thoughts in letters to an imaginary friend. The reason she needs this sort of companion is that in real life no one exists in whom she can confide utterly. Early in her diary, Anne reveals her flaws of chattering, resenting her mother and sisters, and upsetting others by her immature behavior. She also displays a rebellious attitude toward criticism and correction from adults, especially since she does not see in them the examples she would like to follow. Her resentment of her mother in the early stages of the diary is mostly the result of an Oedipal rivalry for the love of her father. Her attitude toward Margot is the result of a natural sibling rivalry. Anne has little desire to emulate her older sister's qualities of intelligence, good behavior, and good looks; instead she wishes to be loved as an individual on her own merits. Anne feels that her sister ignores her and that her mother is not competent to understand her. So she withdraws from them and seeks solace in her father's affection and approval.

Having been cut off from the natural outlets of friends, school, sports, and entertainment, Anne is forced inward and finds her chief occupations in the early months of hiding to be self-criticism, analysis, and justification. She is an emotionally and intellectually sensitive girl whose understanding exceeds her experience. Forced into an uncomfortable situation by the emergency living arrangement, Anne finds it difficult to achieve the self-control necessary to get along with the others and at the same time maintain her independence. Her desire for acceptance conflicts with her equal need to excel and be recognized. Her theories do not always find compatibility with her actions because of the strain of such confined living.

As strongly as she criticizes the others, she is equally harsh with herself. She is an idealist whose sensitivity often causes her to feel rejected and alone in her valiant attempt to be good. By the same token, she rejects the others on the grounds of their imperfections. But more important is the fact that because she is in adolescence, she cannot always account either to herself or others for her extremes of mood and inconsistent behavior. Hence, she withdraws into herself, feeling that if anyone can understand her it is she alone. Months of trying with mixed results bring Anne to a greater understanding of her former and present selves. She is aware of her previous childishness and present maturity but has not found her introverted life satisfying. Her major discovery after the first year is that she is passionately lonely.

Having outgrown some of her self-centered patterns of behavior, she is ready to try relating to the others in a new way. She will restrain herself at all costs, even when she knows she is faking an attitude of concession. To her surprise and wry pleasure, the new method works. She has ceased to resent her mother for the old reasons, has learned to love her father in a different, less dependent way, and has begun to perceive her sister as a less remote creature who might be a girl with needs and feelings similar to her own although manifested differently.

Having suffered intensely the worst aspects of "growing pains," Anne feels an almost smug sense of her own independence and self-reliance. Realizing that her sudden growing up was probably precipitated by the effects of the war, she resents the concentrated anguish it caused her but appreciates her new maturity for the power it gives her. This power is rooted in self-knowledge, from which develops a new and more sympathetic attitude toward the others. Expecting more from herself, she demands less from those about her. She understands their failings because she has come to terms with her own. Her life is conducted on a more realistic basis. Yet she has remained firm in her ideals, realizing that only strong faith, courage, and hope will see her through these dark moments that she knows she must experience alone. A sense of guilt hovers over her reflections of past behavior, but she is determined to reestablish her relationships on a more mature level.

With all her introspective activity and the satisfaction gained by her inner struggle, she is still disturbed by an unremitting loneliness and the need to give and receive affection. As the relationship she seeks cannot be conducted with a member of her family or with one of the other adults, she transfers her idealized image of Peter Schiff from her memory to Peter van Daan. Because of her growing emotional and physical maturity, it necessarily follows a pattern of affection that is more than a friendship but less than love. Having found a love object, Anne is now secure enough to drop many of her leftover defenses. This is manifested in her latest attitude toward others, which shows more humility and compassion coupled with more courage and tact in asserting her independence as a young adult. Yet Anne is not without her problems. She is still moody and frequently disappointed in herself and others. Much of this dissatisfaction comes from without, for the war and life in hiding have affected Anne as well as the others.

In summary, Anne is exceptionally intelligent, courageous, honest, forthright, able to understand others and herself, eager for perfection, and willing to work hard. She is also difficult and temperamental at times and can be tactless and quite stubborn.

## MARGOT

In contrast to Anne, Margot is less outspoken, more mature, and more reserved. She is intelligent but more disciplined and directed into narrower fields of scholarly interest. Aware of her younger sister's sensitivity and often hostile attitude, Margot ignores Anne to avoid increasing their rivalry. Occasionally she defends herself with a caustic or catty remark. More inclined to be like her mother, Margot seeks the companionship of Mrs. Frank in preference to that of her father. Because she is older, she is better able to understand her mother's problems. In addition, Margot and her mother seem to have similar reactions to situations. Margot, too, suffers from loneliness and fear caused by the war, but hers is a quiet desperation manifested in poor sleep and appetite, extreme fatigue, and self-containment. As Anne matures, Margot extends the hand of friendship, sensing Anne's need for a confidante. She is much less timid in her approach to Anne than vice versa. Margot understands Anne far better than the younger girl realizes, yet she does not force herself upon her sister when Anne withdraws. Margot is exceedingly gracious and wise in her reaction to Anne's and Peter's relationship. Margot complains little and endures much. In this way, she is a great deal like her father.

## MRS. FRANK

A woman from a background of wealth and culture, Mrs. Frank is attractive, literate, and accustomed to a comfortable life. She has a progressive outlook on parenthood, considering her daughters more as friends than subordinate offspring. As a rival with her younger daughter for the love of Mr. Frank, she attempts to reach Anne through the only kind of love she can offer. Rejected, she turns for solace and companionship to her older daughter, Margot. Trusting her husband to see Anne through this Oedipal phase, Mrs. Frank cannot resist continued attempts to secure Anne's love but failing to do so often retaliates by reprimanding the young girl. A fairly intense woman whose background has not prepared her for the hardships inflicted by the war, Mrs. Frank suffers initially from shock and fear in the new quarters. Once a pattern of living has been established, she complies as far as possible with what is expected of her, often leaning, however, on Mrs. van Daan to perform the more menial tasks. Rarely complaining but showing the effects of war in much the same ways as Margot, Mrs. Frank bears the burden of the war with forced calm and controlled silence. The relationship between Mr. and Mrs. Frank is rarely marred by disagreements or outbursts. Those that do arise are usually the result of Anne's offensiveness toward her mother, to which the older woman reacts with tears and an appeal to her husband for help. Her role is that of dependence on her husband, who protects her with wisdom and affection, often shielding her from anything upsetting. Mrs. Frank's strength of character is of a dependent rather than independent nature, and she can be relied on for endurance and sympathy, trust and compassion, so long as she herself feels protected.

## MR. FRANK

A man of courage and foresight, Mr. Frank has planned far in advance how he will protect his family from Nazism. He has been the organizer of an elaborate underground arrangement whereby he can remain in Holland, keep his family safe, and indirectly guide his business. Born into wealth and culture, Mr. Frank is a man of the world who utilizes courage and intelligence against unfavorable odds. His intellect and sensitivity are great sources of strength. He is judicious, looked on by the others as leader, peacemaker, and confidant. He never openly reveals his troubles but contains them as well as the problems of others. His suffering is made evident only by certain facial expressions or detachment into his intellectual pursuits. His relationships are strained by others' intense dependence on him. He is able to cope with family difficulties by distributing his loyalty and affection equally among his wife and two daughters, although it seems that Anne requires extra attention and care. Occasionally, he seems to take Anne's part when she might have learned more from handling a situation alone.

## PETER VAN DAAN

Throughout most of the period in hiding, Peter is shy, awkward, and intent on keeping to himself. His relationship with his parents seems to be relatively free from strife. The occasional instances in which he is disciplined do not seem to indicate extraordinary misbehavior on his part or undue harshness on his parents' side. Peter displays manliness and courage in attending to the patrol and inspection duties assigned to him. His affection is expressed by his love for his cat, Mouschi, and the office cat, Boche. His attempts to express affection for the others seems to be limited by adolescent awkwardness. He is reasonably intelligent but has neither the drive nor the discipline for studies displayed by

Anne and Margot. As an outlet for the pressures of confined living, he sleeps a great deal, stays alone, and often lets off steam in solitary outbursts of profanity in the attic. He appears to be cordial and well mannered. When annoyed, he either retreats or becomes tongue-tied in an attempt to express his anger. He resents having been born a Jew and victimized by Hitler's anti-Semitic legislation. His ambitions for adulthood are uncertain, and he professes a desire to be a gambler or loafer after the war. He is often cynical. In many ways, he is less intellectually curious than Anne, and his interests are more mundane. He scoffs at her ideals and displays a superficial attitude toward life that she finds disconcerting. Much of this may be bluster and an act to make him appear aloof and more masculine, but some of it is genuinely indicative of a characteristic weakness and the desire to make life easy. His dependence on Anne eventually exceeds hers on him, but this is most likely the effect of first love on a young man who has never before opened himself to anyone. Peter is gentle and discreet with Anne, never taking physical or emotional advantage of their relationship.

## MRS. VAN DAAN

A woman of different background from that of Anne's mother, Mrs. van Daan tends to be more open in her emotions, often to the distress of others. She is flirtatious, vain, and often petty. She tends to be more hysterical in her reactions to the effects of the war, often suffering acutely from strange delusions of harm and death. On the other hand, she has a warmth and generosity that is easily displayed if properly encouraged. Mrs. van Daan is much more domestically capable than Mrs. Frank and undertakes more than her share of the household duties. Her intelligence is rather limited, and she often says things that display her lack of wisdom and that amuse the others. She tends also to be more old-fashioned in her outlook on childrearing than the progressive Franks and expresses gratuitous opinions on this and other topics, often causing more disagreement among the others than is necessary. She is somewhat jealous of Anne because of the girl's superior intelligence and her ability to draw Peter into her confidence. However, she is often the one Anne can discuss things with openly if the topic is not too controversial.

## MR. VAN DAAN

Seemingly a competent man, Mr. van Daan is noted for his general reliability and willingness to undertake his share of responsibility. He tends to be stubborn and considers his opinions irrefutable. He is a stern but loving father to Peter. His relationship with his wife is marred by coarse, loud bickering, which both seem to thrive upon. He does not display a particularly keen intellect, but he is well informed in general matters and enjoys talking politics. He seems to be rather firmly constituted and is able to withstand many pressures but becomes particularly unnerved by short cigarette rations and complains readily when he does not feel well.

## MR. DUSSEL

An older man, childless, and lonesome for the woman he used to live with, Mr. Dussel often exhibits a peevishness and desire to be let alone. He is often inconsiderate. On the other hand, he has the ability to remove himself from the quarrels of the others as he finds their outbursts detestable and unnerving. He is critical, particularly of the young. He is somewhat of an "Old World gentleman," retaining certain formalities that add a touch of grandeur not only to his personality but also to the lives of the others. He seeks for the most part to be uninvolved, finding solitude and comfort in the mysterious work projects that take up most of his waking hours. He is not sympathetic to others' problems, finding it easier to ignore them than become involved at the expense of forfeiting his aloofness. When he does become involved in squabbles, his intense discomfort in such situations causes him to act pedantic and childishly unreasonable. He is also capable of graciousness and a limited amount of compassion, although it is apparent that in his lonesomeness he is becoming somewhat bitter.

## MINOR CHARACTERS

### MIEP AND JAN GIES

A devoted couple in the employ of Mr. Frank, they are solid, reliable, and loyal to their Jewish friends. Their willingness to work tirelessly and to take risks indicates the high caliber of their characters. They are typical of the Dutch underground, whose unselfish acts of loyalty and courage earned the entire world's admiration.

### BEP VOSKUIJL

A woman in her early twenties employed as a secretary in Mr. Frank's business, Bep is another courageous, loyal member of the Dutch underground. She, too, is unselfishly devoted to those in hiding, working hard and spending her nerves in faithful service spread too thin among her responsibilities to her job, father, fiancé, and eight Jewish friends.

### KUGLER AND KLEIMAN

Friends and business associates of long standing, these men are the mainstays of Mr. Frank's commercial and personal interests. Bearing more than their share of responsibility takes its toll on Kugler's nerves and Kleiman's physical condition, but they are tirelessly loyal and hard working to the very end. For their activities in the Dutch underground, both were sentenced by the Nazis to serve terms in Dutch concentration camps. Both men returned alive after the liberation of Holland to bear testimony against the Nazis.

# ESSAY QUESTIONS AND ANSWERS

***Question***

Anne is often disturbed about her relationship with her parents. In what way does her attitude mature toward both her father and her mother?

***Answer***

When we first meet Anne she is going through what is known as the "Oedipal" stage, manifested in the resentment she displays toward her mother and her preference for her father. At this point Anne is her mother's rival for Mr. Frank's love. There are many ways that Anne excludes her mother from her affections. Among them are frequent instances of refusal to communicate with her mother, either by ignoring her offers of companionship, by arguing with whatever Mrs. Frank says about her behavior, or by excluding her mother from her confidence. Anne prefers to rely on her father for correction, companionship, and comfort. As she begins to feel ashamed of her attitude toward her mother, Anne examines the reasons for it. She comes to the conclusion that Mrs. Frank is a poor example of motherhood, especially since the woman considers her daughters more as friends, thereby failing to achieve the maternal authority and distinction that are the proper attributes of a mother in Anne's mind. Anne also feels that her mother is too frequently out of sorts and takes these moods out on her. Anne resolves to alienate herself permanently from her mother and to strive for total love and approval from her father. Discovering that the bond of love that exists between her parents is one she cannot damage, Anne withdraws from them both and feels deserted. She is determined to do her growing up by herself now. Ashamed of her own resentment, Anne attempts to feign a response to her parents even though she does not actually feel the warmth she displays. When she discovers that her parents' attitude is consistent and that hers is the one undergoing a change, she does some more serious thinking and analyzes the situation again, giving particular consideration to her mother. The result is that Anne begins to perceive her mother as an individual with human shortcomings as well as some good qualities. She does regret, however, that her mother is not the ideal model hat she herself would like to follow. By the same token, Anne realizes that her father can never belong to her alone. In fact, now that she has Peter as a love object, she no longer wants her father in the old way. Caring for Peter has helped Anne realize how her mother must care for her father. This helps her to identify with womanliness and causes her to be less resentful of her mother and other women. It is also possible now for Anne to understand the personality differences between herself and her mother, and in so doing she can accept the good and adjust to the bad qualities. Moreover, she no longer tries to force her mother into an ideal image that fails to live up to her former concept of perfection. With her parents in a more realistic perspective, Anne finds her relationships with both greatly improved.

***Question***

How do the members of this group in hiding fight the pressures of confined living? Whose methods are most successful and why?

***Answer***

Since the occupants of the hiding place have been cut off from the customary forms of entertainment, their only available outlets are listening to the radio, conversing, participating in domestic chores, and engaging in limited gymnastic exercises. The women are able to knit, sew, and clean; the young people have their learning activities; and the men may attend to security and those few affairs of business for which they are still responsible. Nevertheless, the routine of sameness becomes unbearably boring, and only extreme efforts of positive thinking make any activity seem worthwhile. Too much thinking causes depression by drawing personalities into themselves with self-pity and despair over their plight. It is necessary for each person to find something to do of special interest. For Anne, the hobbies she has acquired are very helpful. They include tracing the lineage of European royal families, collecting pictures of film stars, learning different languages, practicing shorthand, helping with Bep's office work, and writing in her diary. This last project, while valuable as an outlet for her emotions, often causes her to reflect even more unhappily on her problems. Margot pursues pretty much the same pattern of intellectual activity as Anne and finds an outlet in her mother's companionship. Peter has his cats, on whom he showers affection, and his studies and chores, and he manages to sleep off much of the frustrations of confined living. Mrs. Frank reads a great deal, sews, and finds comfort in her relationship with her husband and her older daughter. Mr. Frank has so much responsibility that he is often kept busier than his nerves can stand. His outlets are translating Dickens from English into German, working with his daughters on their rojects, reading classical German drama aloud to those who wish to listen, and dabbling at poetry. Mr. van Daan spends a good deal of time keeping up with all sources of war information, studying maps, and working out theories of war strategy and politics. Mrs. van Daan's chief occupation is attending to domestic matters. Such activities as scrubbing, cooking, and cleaning help rid her of nervous energy. Mr. Dussel has an important project, which most likely concerns dental science.

Those best able to utilize their mental resources have the advantage over those whose outlets are manual or primarily physical. The better able one is to devote oneself to a subject of study, the easier it is to keep away unwanted thoughts. Mr. Frank seems to be the most adept at mental escape, and Dussel is likely the next. Margot and Mrs. Frank are fairly well able to live with their own thoughts when not engaged in deliberate mental labor. Anne's imagination takes her out of herself, but as often as not lands her in a nest of problems equally as disturbing as the ones she left behind. For both Anne and Peter, the best outlet is their relationship, but that comes very late in the course of their life in hiding. Mr. and Mrs. van Daan seem to have the least intellectual interests and for that reason often fall to bickering and complaining.

***Question***

What are the sources of unpleasantness among the eight occupants of the hideout? How can they be explained and possibly condoned?

***Answer***

The sources of unpleasantness among the eight people in hiding can be divided into those common to all and others that are individual matters. The common sources of unpleasantness are numerous and understandable. The limitations of space make privacy and freedom of physical movement almost impossible. The sameness of routine is frustrating. Reports of the arrests, deportations and deaths of Jews are extremely bad for morale. Many of their friends and acquaintances are victims of Nazi persecution. The air raids are nerve-racking and prevent sleep. Bombings nearby create terror because all realize there is no such thing as escape. Rations of food and other commodities fluctuate, often from bad to worse. The fear of being discovered is always present and made more real by frequent burglaries and suspicious people nearby. When illness strikes, a doctor may never be summoned, and the home remedies relied on take longer to effect cures. The general morale is subject to constant fluctuation, depending on radio broadcasts of war news.

Individual problems are as difficult to solve as to live with. Personalities conflict: Mrs. Frank against Anne, Dussel versus Mr. van Daan, Mrs. van Daan versus Mrs. Frank, Mr. and

Mrs. van Daan against each other, Anne versus Margot, and the van Daan family against the Franks. Certain habits of one person annoy the entire group: Mrs. van Daan's girlishness and hysteria, Anne's chattering and know-all attitude, Mr. Dussel's peevishness, and Mr. van Daan's stubbornness. There is no day completely free of internal strife. Everyone longs to be free; the present is dismal and the future uncertain.

***Question***

In what ways do the other seven members of the group in hiding deal with Anne's precociousness, and what are possible reasons for their reactions?

***Answer***

Anne's superior intellect, astute perception, and emotional sensitivity create problems for the others. Her father responds wisely and lovingly, accepting his daughter's precociousness more as a challenge than as a burden. Mrs. Frank's occasional harshness toward Anne grows out of a need to defend herself in their subtle rivalry for Mr. Frank's love. Margot seems to ignore her younger sister, finding Anne's immaturities annoying and her advanced ideas not always of interest. Dussel is flabbergasted by Anne as the product of progressive methods of upbringing. He is overwhelmed by her mental and physical energy. He ignores her whenever possible and criticizes her when combat becomes inevitable. Peter comes to admire her humor, intelligence, and outward self-confidence. Mr. and Mrs. van Daan see Anne's precociousness as poor behavior resulting from a progressive upbringing. They seem unaware of her extraordinary qualifications for the most part and interpret her words and actions negatively. Mrs. van Daan is apt to feel intellectually inferior to Anne, and Mr. van Daan is aware of her low opinion of his stubbrnness. Thus threatened, both react to her with criticism. Later on, she seeks the van Daans on a level that makes for certain areas of compatibility and gains their moderate admiration for her superior qualities.

### *Question*

How does Anne's independent spirit develop from outbursts of childish rebelliousness to mature self-reliance?

### *Answer*

From her prehiding days at the Jewish Lyceum, Anne's contempt for adult authority has been directly dependent on her concept of ideal beings. If an adult falls short of her image of perfection, then that person's authority will be tested. The only grown-up worthy of authority is her father, who Anne feels is just such an ideal person. For those who do not measure up to Mr. Frank, Anne displays degrees of resentment according to the amount of authority being exercised and the way it is presented. Anne most often obeys, but she questions the purpose of the orders. What she resents most is criticism from those whose own imperfections are obvious to her. It is in this reaction to criticism from her mother, the van Daans, and Dussel that her rebellious outbursts are noticeable. Rather than submit to rebukes and corrections, she attempts to justify herself by mentioning all the reasons she is being unjustly criticized and by pointing out flaws in her accuser. The result is usually calamitous. Feeling herself the victim of unfair criticism, Anne vows to win everyone's respect by a display of perfection and thus gain both independence and recognition as an equal in the eyes of her seniors. For a long period of time Anne withdraws into herself to figure out how she can gain the desired advantage in these relationships without submitting completely to others' points of view or being so offensive in maintaining her own. The result she seeks is one that eventually establishes her as an independent being by giving her self-confidence and less resentment of authority.

Anne succeeds in achieving this independence only after she realizes that it is up to each individual to seek perfection in himself or herself rather than force it on others. When a person is responsible for achieving ideals and does not depend on others to live up to models of perfection, the shortcomings of others can be understood and forgiven. Recognizing this, Anne becomes more realistic in accepting others for what they are while at the same time upholding a pattern of ideals to be followed by herself. Relying less on others and more on herself in this quest for perfection constitutes the source of Anne's mature self-reliance.

***Question***

In what ways does the relationship between Anne and Peter result from a mixture of accident and inevitability?

***Answer***

From Anne's memory comes the strong emotion she felt for Peter Schiff, a friend from her former life on the outside. This emotion is renewed in a dream of such intensity that Anne awakens believing herself in love. That very day she notices Peter van Daan for the first time as a possible object of companionship. As she and Peter get to know one another better, they share their confidences and affections in a relationship that is a mixture of friendship and romance. What has occurred is that Anne, in her longing for a love object, has transferred her attention from the Peter Schiff of her imagination to the Peter van Daan of reality. It is accidental only insofar as he is able to respond to Anne's need. The inevitability lies in Anne's own desire, which was so strong and so intensive that it had to find an object.

***Question***

The five protectors are typical of the Dutch underground movement. What are the factors responsible for their attitude and activity regarding the eight occupants in particular and the "cause" in general?

***Answer***

More than any other European country occupied by the Nazis, the Netherlands is remarkable for the resistance shown by the citizens. The Dutch were particularly resentful of the anti-Semitic legislation enacted by Hitler and sought at first to counteract it by open opposition such as workers' strikes and violent propaganda in print. The Nazis in turn responded with harsh measures: shortening rations, altering the value of money, and restricting privileges of Jews and Christians alike. Afraid of doing further damage to innocent people, anti-Nazi individuals went underground and secretly worked for the destruction of the occupational forces while seeming on the surface to go along with the new rules. Much of their effort was extended to help Jews either to escape or to find safety in hiding. Both methods required breaking the law under close surveillance. Many services were performed for Jews by the sympathizers, such as procuring foreign documents, providing secret shelter, carrying or hiding possessions, and even transporting Jews to safety in other countries.

Motivated by public spirit and private devotion, Miep, Jan, Bep, Kleiman, and Kugler risked their lives daily as they undertook to protect the Franks, van Daans, and Dussel for more than two years. As the protectors had been associated with Mr. Frank's firm for several years, they were trusted with all business and personal matters. In the end Kleiman and Kugler went to Nazi concentration camps in the Netherlands. Miep and Bep found Anne's diary and preserved it for Mr. Frank, the only survivor of the eight in hiding, who eventually had it published.

***Question***

In what way is Anne's diary indicative of her young age? Which aspects reveal a maturity beyond her years?

***Answer***

Anne's youth is apparent in the early pages of her diary in aspects of her style that indicate the awkwardness of a student wrestling with the rules of formal composition and at the same time attempting to free her mind of burdensome thoughts. The formality of her sentence structure negates the freedom of expression she strives for in content. There is, too, a noticeable jumping from topic to topic, producing inconsistencies in tone, point of view, and overall purpose. As the work progresses, however, the writing gains unity. Anne acquires experience in writing, which helps her to lose the early formality that inhibited her wording and flow of ideas. Yet there are still evidences of extremes of mood and tone, which indicate her youthful lack of control. In contrast to these indications of immaturity, Anne's frequent comments on people, the war, and life in general reveal a more mature wisdom and insight.

By the second year, there are more noticeable changes in style and content. Anne's sentences have become more complex in structure. She has also acquired more assurance in handling her content. Another remarkable feature is the development of a more consistent philosophy of life and the obvious formation of a firm set of values. The contradictions appear less as examples of clumsiness than as the expression of Anne's many-faceted personality. In style and in outlook, Anne's work shows growing maturity, often surpassing in depth of thought and honesty the work of many professional writers. Her amazing development took place under conditions of excruciating confinement and the constant threat of death at the hands of the Nazis, and for this reason the *Diary* is considered a triumph of the human spirit.

# CRITICAL COMMENTARY

Eleanor Roosevelt: ". . . A remarkable book. Written by a young girl—and the young are not afraid of telling the truth—it is one of the wisest and most moving commentaries on war and its impact on human beings that I have ever read. Anne Frank's account of the changes wrought upon eight people hiding out from the Nazis for two years during the occupation of Holland, living in constant fear and isolation, imprisoned not only by the terrible outward circumstances of war but inwardly by themselves, made me intimately and shockingly aware of war's greatest evil—the degradation of the human spirit. At the same time, Anne's diary makes poignantly clear the ultimate shining nobility of that spirit."

Meyer Levin: "Anne Frank's diary is too tenderly intimate a book to be frozen with the label 'classic,' and yet no lesser designation serves. For little Anne Frank, spirited, moody, witty, self-doubting, succeeded in communicating in virtually perfect, or classic, form the drama of puberty. But her book is not a classic to be left on the library shelf. It is a warm and stirring confession, to be read over and over for insight and enjoyment. . . . Anne Frank's diary simply bubbles over with amusement, love, discovery. It has its share of disgust, its moments of hatred, but it is so wondrously alive, so near, that one feels overwhelmingly the universalities of human nature. . . . Because the diary was not written in retrospect, it contains the trembling life of every moment—Anne Frank's voice becomes the voice of six million vanished Jewish souls. . . . There is anguish in the thought of how much creative power, how much sheer beauty of living, was cut off through genocide. But through her diary Anne goes on living. . . . Surely she will be widely loved, for this wise and wonderful young girl brings back a poignant delight in the infinite human spirit."

Albert Goes: "Now and then in the course of our life we meet a girl like Anne Frank—not too often, for the level of intelligence, reflectiveness, depth of feeling, and precocity and are revealed in the jottings of this thirteen-or fourteen-year-old are certainly extraordinary. But her cool, keen observation of human beings, and her resolve to be alert to the comic element in even the worst situations, these are familiar to us. . . . We have her diary still, and in that journal a most remarkable document of awakening humanity written down quite without premeditation, and for that very reason absolutely sincere. . . . It is necessary that this voice be heard in the world [today], which has not ceased to be a world of concentration camps and persecutions. And one must be ever grateful to the two Hollanders who, in that room ransacked by the Secret Police, hid and kept secure under magazines and newspapers this child's journal—this book that tells the truth without a trace of false ornament, tells the whole truth and nothing but the truth."

Ann Birstein and Alfred Kazin: "To everything that happened to her, to everything that she felt, Anne gave a kind of permanence by transcribing it, and day after day she went on adding still another segment to the world she was creating. . . . In her diary, where her subject chose her, its vividness and poignance are overwhelming. . . . What makes her achievement really amazing is how little, aside from her own natural gifts of observation and her sense of humor, she had to work with. Other people have countrysides and multitudes. For Anne, the one boy upstairs was love; a single chestnut tree seen from her window, nature; a patch of blue sky—heaven. . . . Anne Frank has become a universal legend. Out of the millions who were gassed, burned, shot, hanged, starved, tortured, buried alive, the young girl who died so 'peacefully' in Bergen-Belsen, almost in unconscious sympathy with her dead sister Margot, has become a prime symbol of the innocence of all those who died in the middle of the twentieth century at the hands of the most powerful state in western Europe. Perhaps more than any of the known dead, and certainly more than the now nameless ones who died scratching the ceilings of the gas chambers in the last agonized struggle against death, [Anne Frank] has become the personal example of the heartlessness, the bestiality, the still unbelievable cruelty of Germans in World War II. Upon her, at least all agree; in her all peoples, in the uneasy peace since 1945 that is no peace, can find a moment's occasion for compassion and awareness. . . . *The Diary of a Young Girl* survived its author and most of her family, as it has already survived so many books about the war, because the faithfulness with which it records an unusual experience reminds us—as opposition to Nazism on its own terms never can—of the sweetness and goodness that are possible in a world where a few souls still have good will. The *Diary* moves us because its author had the strength to see, to remember, to hope."

Ilya Ehrenburg: "This is not a novel by a celebrated author, it is the diary of a thirteen-year-old girl; but it affects the reader more profoundly than many masterly works of literature. Everyone knows that the Hitlerites killed six million Jews, the citizens of twenty countries, rich and poor, famous and unknown. . . . Six million were poisoned in gas chambers, shot in ravines or against fortress walls, condemned to slow death by starvation. They were separated from the world by the walls of ghettos, by the barbed wire of concentration camps. Nobody knows what they felt and thought. One voice speaks for six million—the voice not of a sage or a poet but of an ordinary little girl. . . . Millions of readers know Anne Frank as if she had been to their homes. Six million perfectly innocent people perished. One clear, child's voice lives on: it has proved stronger than death."

Garsaon Kanin: Anne Frank "remains for us ever a shining star, a radiant presence who, during her time of terror and humiliation and imprisonment, was able to find it in herself to write in her immortal diary, 'In spite of everything, I still believe that people are good at heart.' Her unlived life challenge[s] humanity to rise to her faith."

Stefan Kanfer: "There is, of course, no way to determine what kind of writer Anne Frank might have become. Child sacrifice is a tragedy beyond words, and it scarcely matters whether a genius or an ordinary citizen perished in the Holocaust. It is only certain that her final volume is a testimony to a green talent and a mature spirit. Each page refreshingly repeats the invaluable moral lesson of her diary: if it is implausible to bid farewell to anguish, it is impossible to close the book on hope."

# BIBLIOGRAPHY


Berryman, John. "The Development of Anne Frank." In *The Freedom of the Poet.* New York: Farrar, Straus, 1976.

Bettelheim, Bruno. "The Ignored Lesson of Anne Frank." In *Surviving and Other Essays.* New York: Knopf, 1979.

Birstein, Ann, and Alfred Kazin. "Introduction." In *The Works of Anne Frank.* New York: Doubleday, 1959.

Bullock, Alan. *Hitler: A Study in Tyranny.* New York: Harper, 1964.

Dawidowicz, Lucy S. *The Holocaust Reader.* New York, 1976.

———. *The War Against the Jews 1933–1945.* New York: Holt, 1985.

Ehrenburg, Ilya. "Anne Frank's Diary." In *Chekhov, Stendhal, and Other Essays.* New York: Knopf, 1963.

Fogelman, Eva. *Conscience & Courage: Rescuers of Jews During the Holocaust.* New York: Anchor Books, 1994.

Frank, Anne. *The Diary of a Young Girl.* The Definitive Edition. Ed. Otto H. Frank and Mirjam Pressler. Trans. Susan Massotty. New York: Anchor Books, 1995.

Gies, Miep. *Anne Frank Remembered.* New York: Simon & Schuster, 1987.

Goldhagen, Daniel Jonah. *Hitler's Willing Executioners: Ordinary Germans and the Holocaust.* New York: Knopf, 1996.

Hartman, Geoffrey H., ed. *Holocaust Remembrance: The Shapes of Memory.* Cambridge, MA: Blackwell, 1994.

Kanin, Garson. "Anne Frank at 50." *Newsweek,* vol. 92, no. 26, June 25, 1979.

Levin, Meyer. "The Child Behind the Secret Door." *New York Times Book Review,* June 15, 1952.

Lindwer, Willy. *Last Seven Months of Anne Frank.* New York: Pantheon, 1991.

Pommer, Henry F. "The Legend and Art of Anne Frank." *Judaism,* vol. 9, no. 1, Winter 1960.

Roosevelt, Eleanor. "Introduction." In *The Diary of a Young Girl.* New York: Doubleday, 1952.

Schnabel, Ernest. *Anne Frank: A Portrait in Courage.* New York: Harcourt, 1958.

Shirer, William L. *The Rise and Fall of Adolf Hitler.* New York: Random House, 1961.

Steenmeijer, Anna G., ed. *A Tribute to Anne Frank.* New York: Doubleday, 1971.

Yahil, Leni. *The Holocaust: The Fate of European Jewry, 1932–1945.* New York: Oxford University Press, 1990.

# NOTES

# NOTES

# NOTES

# NOTES

# NOTES

# NOTES

# NOTES

# NOTES

# NOTES